HOW TO PUTT BETTER THAN YOU'VE EVER IMAGINED USING THE PERFECT PLUMB BOB METHOD

The Definitive Guide to Golf's Most Mysterious & Misunderstood Putting Tip: Plumb Bobbing

Dr. Terry Zachary

Dr. Terry Zachary

doczac Enterprises Inc.

114 - 1124 Fir Ave Blaine, WA,

USA 98230

Email: terry@doczac.com

Ordering Information:

Book sales by corporations, associations, and others; Orders by U.S./International trade bookstores, retailers and wholesalers, contact the author at the address above.

How To Putt Better Than You've Ever Imagined Using The Perfect Plumb Bob Method: The Definitive Guide To Golf's Most Mysterious & Misunderstood Putting Tip – Plumb Bobbing / Dr. Terry Zachary.

Paperback

ISBN: 978-1-7772335-0-1

Category: 1. Sports: Golf

Dedication

This book is dedicated to curious golfers everywhere, as well to my wife, Rhonda, and children, Jackson, Jonah, and Emily who put up with me as I finalized this personal passion project, and to my brother, Darryl and mom, Marlene, who always encouraged me to follow my interests.

TABLE OF CONTENTS

Please visit www.6footer.com to compliment the information gained within The Perfect Plumb Bob Method.

INTRODUCTION

The concept of bobbing for apples still puzzles me to this day. Why are kids asked to do it? Why *do* kids do it? Why did I do it when I was a kid? It seems so unnatural. We have hands, after all. It's no wonder that this activity doesn't continue into adulthood. Bobbing for apples makes no sense to me.

Plumb bobbing to read the slope of a golf green, on the other hand...? —that makes sense *to me!* In fact, it is clear as day *to me.*

I also realize that my view is not so common currently for the many people who play the wonderful game of golf. Plumb bobbing is as mysterious as it is misunderstood. It is full of myths and poor advice.

To be clear, plumb bobbing wasn't always logical to me. I had to pick it apart for many years to arrive at my current opinion—which is: I believe it is as useful of a technique as there is for determining slope in golf. Plumb bobbing is my #1 tool for reading greens.

The Perfect Plumb Bob Method book aims to set the record straight regarding 'how to-,' 'why to-,' and 'when to-' plumb bob so that every golfer can gain an advantage like they've never imagined in regard to reading greens. When you are virtually sure how a putt breaks, you can make equally confident putt plans and putting strokes.

And you make a ton of putts!

The pages to follow will give you a comprehensive grasp on The Perfect Plumb Bob Method, as well as how to process the information that you collect.

The Perfect Plumb Bob Method is referred to as *'Perfect'* in regards to the detailed preparation process that is essential to read slope. Follow each step properly, practise and commit to habit, and you'll start to see details revealed about putt paths and slope that will astound you.

About The Author

Throughout my career, I was fairly successful at every level of golf – *in general terms*. I won a lot of tournaments as an amateur and as a college golfer. I played professionally for just under four years, and was *moderately-to-quite* competitive, if that is a category.

I worked hard. I studied hard. I progressed well.

Unfortunately, their came a point where the years necessary to solidify my ascent into top level professional golf appeared to be too many. In essence, I was not good enough to make a living, and the evidence was meek that I ever would.

To build a career as a professional tournament golfer demands a rank of well roundedness that is hard to imagine. Grit, skill, strength, commitment, aggressiveness, calm, intelligence, health, fight, touch and patience—all at a world-class level—are rarely mentioned in the same sentence. Professional golf demands them all.

That said, I feel I had many of those attributes in my game; a few were simply not developed to the extent required.

For example, I might be the only person who has played high-level amateur golf, college golf and professional golf who has *never had a hole-in-one*. Not one. It used to bother me to no end. I loathed the topic when someone brought it up. And my buddies always did... and still do. I don't blame them. I would do the same to them if roles were reversed. It has certainly kept me grounded.

Ask your golf professional (or if you have a friend that is a competitive professional player) how many pros they know who have had *no* holes-in-one. I mean *zero*. The number is likely small, if any. I have friends who have 6, 8, 9, even double digits. And it's not like I'm an unlucky person. What you might conclude about this career hole-in-one statistic is that I was a pretty mediocre iron player. You'd be right.

Now I hope I *don't get a hole-in-one*! It would *wreck my marketing*.

You might wonder how did I stayed competitive? I've thought about that myself many times and believe I've come up with the most probable answer: I was an extremely good putter. And to be a good putter, you have to be able to read greens *well*. *Very well*.

Most golfers *want* to be good putters, but don't spend any time on its main prerequisite: *reading greens*.

The main staple I depended on for reading greens eventually became *plumb bobbing*. Early in my golf career, I used plumb bobbing as a *final check* on my reads. As I became more competitive (and more consistent at plumb bobbing), the plumb bob became my *go-to* tool.

I knew players who could see break and slope in greens better than me. It frustrated the heck out of me. I worked hard to catch up. Seeing break seemed to be an innate talent. They were good. I was average. It just *was*.

3

That all changed when I truly figured out the plumb bob. Those who did plumb bob didn't seem to know what they were doing. Or they couldn't explain it. Or both. Thus, I figured it out in my own. And the details were tricky.

Studying the neurology of balance as a health care professional helped a great deal. Once I understood it, I realized that plumb bobbing was not an innate gift of the few; it was a science that could be learned by all.

Over the years I've come to realize how full of myths, misunderstandings, judgments and egos the world of plumb bobbing is filled with. Such a shame because plumb bobbing, done correctly, can remove so many burdens that hinder putting success.

In hindsight, I related positively with plumb bobbing on the golf course as a result of three main experiential chapters in my life— I never waivered from trying to learn it.

The first was from working in concrete as a young kid with my stepfather, Carl Lind. He and my stepbrothers, Darrell & Trevor, seemed to have such an easy grasp on what horizontal level was. Through repetition, they just appeared to, again, *get it*. That always intrigued me.

I remember many times throughout my life when I felt *I was getting it*, but never really had the physical proof to assure myself. When I did put a level up to what my eye saw, I could see I was still *off*.

Too bad the Rules of Golf restrict the use of a carpenter's level on the greens. That would have saved me a lot of trouble.

Later, as a young adult, I owned and worked regularly on the structures of a horse barn, complete with an indoor arena. That was my second strong reminder of the importance of *plumb*. I was again reminded that knowing perfect, unquestionable vertical (and thus horizontal) is very useful in applications other than golf.

My third life experience chapter that solidified the importance of knowing vertical came in my career as a sports and family chiropractor. In my practise, I worked with a vertical string plumb line and eventually an *Anatometer*, which stressed the importance of vertical center in the human frame.

Spinal posture (and the body's reaction to its own vertical center) is indeed one of the most under-rated concepts in human health. Under-monitored, under-checked, under-noticed, and under-popularized by the media, our population's understanding of center of gravity is, generally, *not very good.*

We understand that groceries get heavier as we carry them further from the center of our body, but we don't understand that our body parts *weigh differently, work differently,* and *wear differently* when our body is not balanced on its own natural vertical center.

Poor posture is rampant in our world. We don't realize that our spines protect our delicate spinal cords, which carry vital nerve messages for life, health and coordination between the brain and the rest of the body—back and forth—every nanosecond of every day.

When our posture suffers subtly, our health and performance suffers greatly. When our posture suffers greatly, well…

In my opinion, every human being should know his or her center of gravity reading as readily as their blood pressure. Posture is *that central* to one's personal health expression.

Let's just say that vertical, and the vertical center of the body, has been a constant interest of mine—for decades. In golf (through plumb bobbing, reading putts), in building (walls, floors and maintenance) and in health care (analyzing my own and my patients' potential for stability and function), I have come to see the deep benefits of understanding this constant of nature known as *gravity.*

It is a lifetime goal of mine to maintain my body on its vertical center, to maintain the drainage of my backyard, and to hang wall art so that it is appealingly level. Plus, I will use The Perfect Plumb Bob Method in every round of golf I ever play.

I've played golf virtually all my life (since about 14). It's a fun game, an educational game, a physical, mental and emotional game. It's a great game. As one gets better at golf, it's the type of game that's difficult to get *even better at*—if that makes any sense. Improvement is reasonable, until its not.

To continue to improve at golf, the devil is in the details. To progress, one must learn as much as one can about the natural laws that relate to the game. Next, one must put that knowledge to work habitually to build unshakable neuromuscular pathways.

It takes time and focused effort to get good at golf, and that's why golf may be slowing in popularity with younger people. Very little guaranteed instant gratification, lots of hard work, and payoffs that come *eventually.* That's a tough sell nowadays.

Golf is the best game in the world in my opinion for these very reasons. Golf mimics life.

I played professional golf in the mid 90's, and had much of the information to follow in my head at that time. I also thought plumb bobbing was more universally well understood. It is not. And it requires clear instruction to have a chance at *getting it.* What starts as *confusing* is soon *easy,* even *intriguing.*

Plumb bobbing is one of the few shortcuts in the game of golf. The Perfect Plumb Bob Method makes golf instantly more gratifying and simpler for any generation of player. That's why I wrote this book.

Since discontinuing my effort at playing professional golf, I have grown a business and began a family. Unfortunately during this decade, I did not make much time for golf. In the few times I did play, the game seemed foreign.

In the last few years, I've started back as if a beginner—which has been both a heartache and a blessing. I missed the game like you miss an old best friend. When you see that person again you immediately take a strong interest in their life.

Like a perennial flower reawakens, my love for the game itself has blossomed again easily. It just needed the sun, water and soil availed to me as my kids and business have grown. More time may be on the horizon for my own deep interests, golf being one of them.

I look forward to teaching many about plumb bobbing. It is perfectly legal, and what likely keeps it legal is that it is passed over by almost everyone. Plumb bobbing is like that fringe school friend who you find to be lovely later in life.

Those golfers who have passed plumb bobbing over have simply not understood it. Thus, it is hard for most golfers to take it seriously. Some guess at it. Few do it. Fewer do it right. Soon, you'll be in the latter category.

There has never been a place to go for plumb bob expertise. There has never been an expert to ask. That all changes with the book ahead as The Perfect Plumb Bob Method holds your hand, step by step.

The Perfect Plumb Bob Method gives golfers invaluable information about the entire structure of each putt, lending information to both line and speed. Once the reader has this information, they have it for life. Gravity never changes.

For the average golfer, The Perfect Plumb Bob Method can easily make a difference of several strokes per round. For the advanced golfer, a few strokes per day in tournaments will explode their resume.

By the end of reading The Perfect Plumb Bob Method book, you will be able to plumb bob properly, and quickly. You will be also be able to observe that so many others do it improperly—*and know why.*

That all said, please don't get arrogant, or think that I am being arrogant. Plumb bobbing is not a perfect science. What The Perfect Plumb Bob Method does is give you a dependable method to gain invaluable and concrete feedback that lends to clear decision making, which in turn leads to the ultimate putting payoff—*confidence.*

Anything that helps take the guesswork out of putting is worth the price of gold to a golfer.

Golfers must understand how plumb bobbing is done to the point where she or he has no doubt about the feedback being gained. The Perfect Plumb Bob Method will do just that and takes the heavy mystique away from this abstract spectacle.

Strap yourself in. Be prepared to get hooked on plumb bobbing and leave all doubts and questions behind. Get used to looking forward to reading putts, making tons of them, and getting strange, suspicious stares from your playing partners.

How would you like *the hole to be scared of you for a change?*

The Perfect Plumb Bob Method will prove that *'if you're not plumb bobbing, you're not trying.'*

It is nature's law, *gravity*, that is front and center in the book to follow. Gravity holds so many secrets for better green reading and putting. It also holds a key for an optimum state of health.

The Perfect Plumb Bob Method to follow will dissect and organize any golfer to be on their way to becoming a green reading master.

Enjoy learning, thinking, practicing, and getting better.

Enjoy growing.

Before you start the book, your first homework assignment: Memorize the acronyms to follow. They will be used *ad naseum*. Learn them now and make the process flow comfortably:

DE – Dominant Eye

VAP – Vertical Alignment Position

NP – Near Point

FP – Far Point

SP – Setup Plane

VL – Vertical Line

LPSP – Lower Putter Shaft Point

UPSP – Upper Putter Shaft Point

Without further adieu, let's bust right into the method, starting with the basics. It's time to become a Perfect Plumb Bobber.

Please visit www.6footer.com to compliment the information
gained within The Perfect Plumb Bob Method.

CHAPTER 1 - DETERMINE YOUR DOMINANT EYE (DE)

Your **Dominant Eye (DE)** will be used as the default site line for all functions going forward in learning, practicing and applying The Perfect Plumb Bob Method. It is super-easy to determine your DE and vitally important to understand. Your DE performs the majority of the function of seeing normally, assisted by its paired weaker eye. You need to know now which is which for yourself.

Let's take a few minutes to determine your DE:

1. Choose a small dot or stationary object 1-3 feet in front of you (Fig 1) on a wall. With both eyes open, extend your arm slightly in front of you (i.e., about 1 foot) and block the object from your vision with your index finger (See Fig 2).

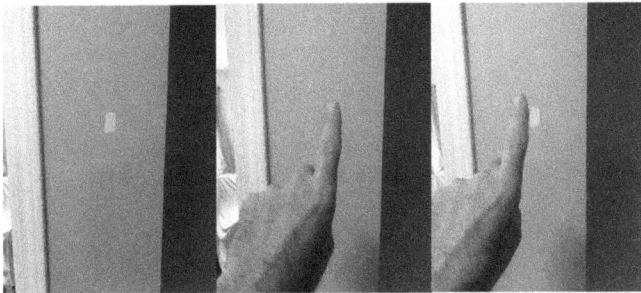

| Fig. 1 | Fig. 2. | Fig. 3 |

11

2. Close one eye. Now the other. When you close your weaker eye, the object will remain hidden behind your finger (Fig. 2). When you close your DE, your finger will shift or *jump* to one side such that the original object is in view (Fig. 3).
3. Your DE is open when the object remains hidden. The eye that is open when the dot or object reappears is your weaker helper eye.

Step 1 is done. That was easy.

This DE exercise is a simple step, but a critically important one as you move forward in your effort to become a Perfect Plumb Bobber. No step is too simple to be overlooked.

Now that you've determined your DE, next you must determine a true vertical from which we *read* the slope of the ground.

CHAPTER 2 - PROPERLY PLUMB YOUR PUTTER

Say that 3 times fast!

There's no way to be effective at plumb bobbing without first understanding how to make your putter *hang plumb* to represent *true vertical*. This is one of the MAIN mistakes golfers make when attempting to plumb bob.

If a golfer is attempting to plumb bob with a non-vertical putter, it will lead to inconsistent and confusing feedback and results. The golfer will eventually conclude that plumb bobbing doesn't work—especially on putts with small, subtle breaks—and they will give up on the process.

When you plumb bob correctly (i.e., *Perfectly*), you'll never give up plumb bobbing.

I've heard experts advise to 'point the toe of the putter down the putt line' such that the 'face is neutral.' In most all cases, that is poor advice—as you'll see from the series of images ahead.

Plumb bobbing works well, if not miraculously. It's the golfer or the golfer's advisor who don't. Thus, all steps to *plumbing* your specific putter *to true vertical* must be well understood and completed.

We will refer now and throughout the book to this aligned position of the putter as the **VAP or Vertical Alignment**

Position. Indeed, all putters can be plumbed to their precise VAP and can thus be used in The Perfect Plumb Blob Method.

Learning to plumb your putter to its VAP is a simple but necessary step, similar to determining your DE. Plus, you will likely find it to be extremely interesting. Every putter is weighted differently (head, neck, shaft, and grip) and every putter head is designed differently. But every mass has a vertical center, including putters.

Fig. 4 Hanging Plumb Line   Fig. 5 Plumb Bob

The first thing you need to do for best results is to set up an actual plumb bob string line (see Fig. 4 & 5) that you can purchase at most hardware stores. The best and easiest place to do this is under a doorframe, yet it can be affixed above any open space. Pro shops and golf teachers can hang a plumb line from a ceiling for regular reference. A brightly colored string is easiest to see and work with. Let the weight and the string settle to dead still. The longer the string is, the better. You now have a true vertical to work with.

True vertical is easily revealed because of gravity. Gravity is natural. Nature never lies and never changes. We humans would be far ahead to understand and utilize nature's blessings as often as possible.

Thanks for the help, gravity!

Start by closing your weak eye and seeing with your DE. Gently hold your putter near the top of the grip by pinching it lightly between your thumb and index or middle finger—whichever is more comfortable (see Fig. 9, 10, 11 and the book cover illustration for general thumb and finger position).

Be sure to hold your putter at the same location on the grip when determining your VAP and when applying your VAP in practise and on the course. Changing your holding location up or down may change the weighting of your putter slightly and affect the VAP.

Hang your putter such that the plumb line is between your putter and your DE. Step back and extend your arm such that you can see the entire putter, top to bottom, easily in one glance.

You will likely notice that your putter shaft does not hang perfectly vertical with the plumb line string at first effort (see Fig. 6). If not, use a trial-and-error progression of rotating your putter until you notice that the middle of the putter shaft aligns perfectly with the string (see Fig. 7). This is the specific VAP for your putter.

It is difficult to miss the VAP because as one continues to rotate the putter past the VAP, you will create a non-vertical angle in the opposite direction (Fig. 8 & 12 are good examples).

Rotate the putter back-and-forth until you determine the rotated position that best fits true vertical, and therefore is that putter's VAP.

Fig. 6 Face Neutral - But Shaft Not Vertical

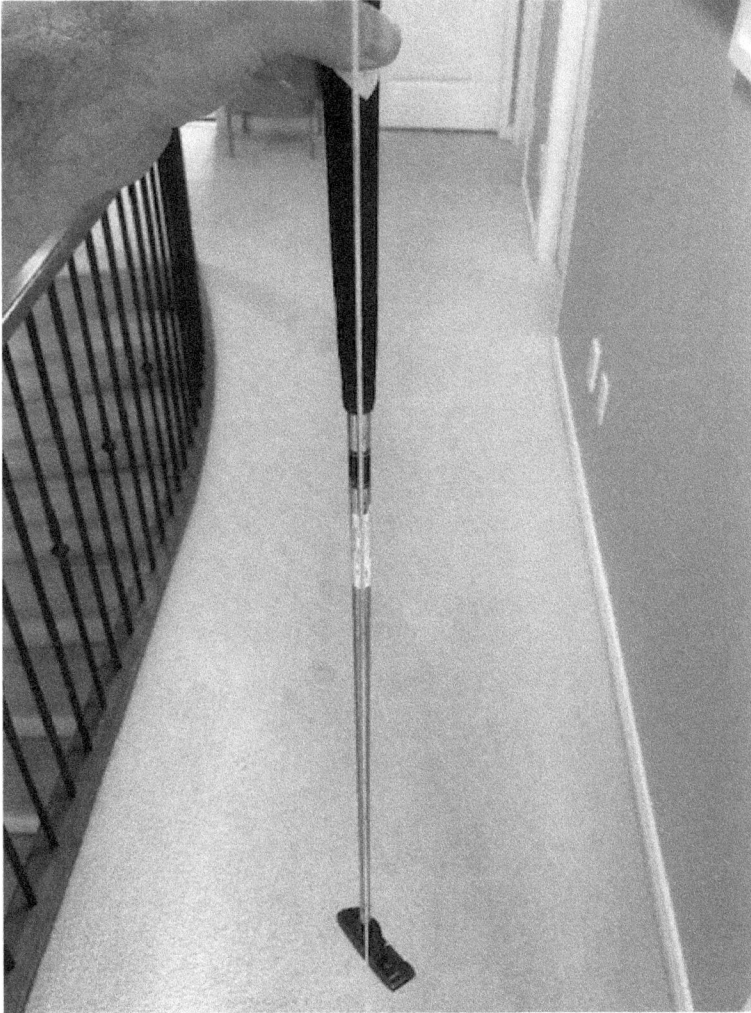

Fig. 7 Vertical Alignement Position - VAP

Fig. 8 Rotated Past Vertical

Refer to Fig 6, 7 & 8 as an example of plumbing one style of putter (blade). To see that another putter style (mallet) plumbs much differently, view Fig. 9, 10, 11 & 12.

Note, this VAP step *can be slightly tricky* as most putter shafts are tapered, not parallel. Thus, the golfer cannot simply line up the *side of the putter shaft* to the hanging plumb string.

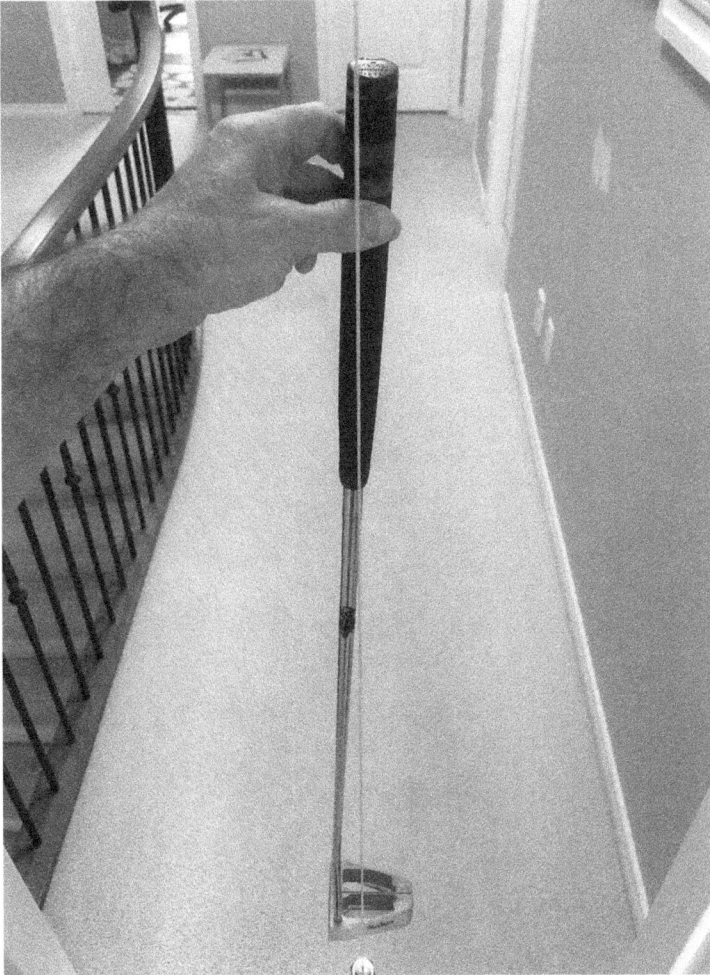

Fig. 9 Face Neutral - But Shaft Not Vertical

Instead, one must align the string *with the center of the putter shaft*. Make sense?

Tapered means that the shaft gets wider as we travel up to the

19

grip.

There is an art to finalizing one's thoughts on where true vertical of the putter shaft exists. Simply repeat the process of trial-and-error rotation until you reach your best conclusion. Do not rush or be hasty. All slopes read going forward will be affected.

Fig. 10 (Not Vertical)

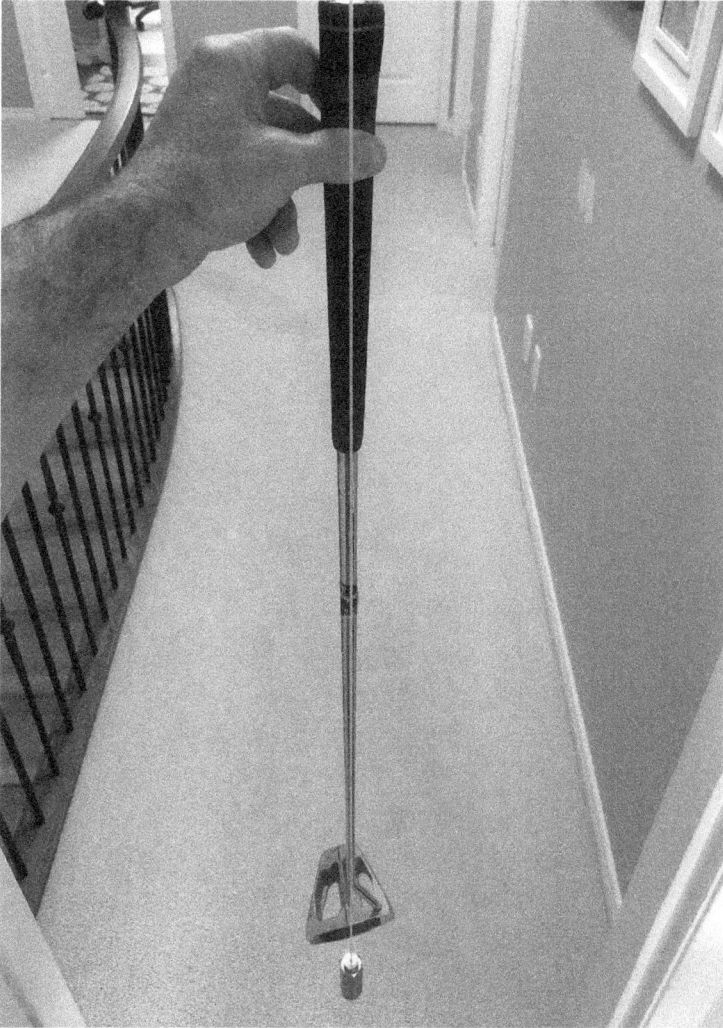

Fig. 11 Vertical Alignement Position - VAP

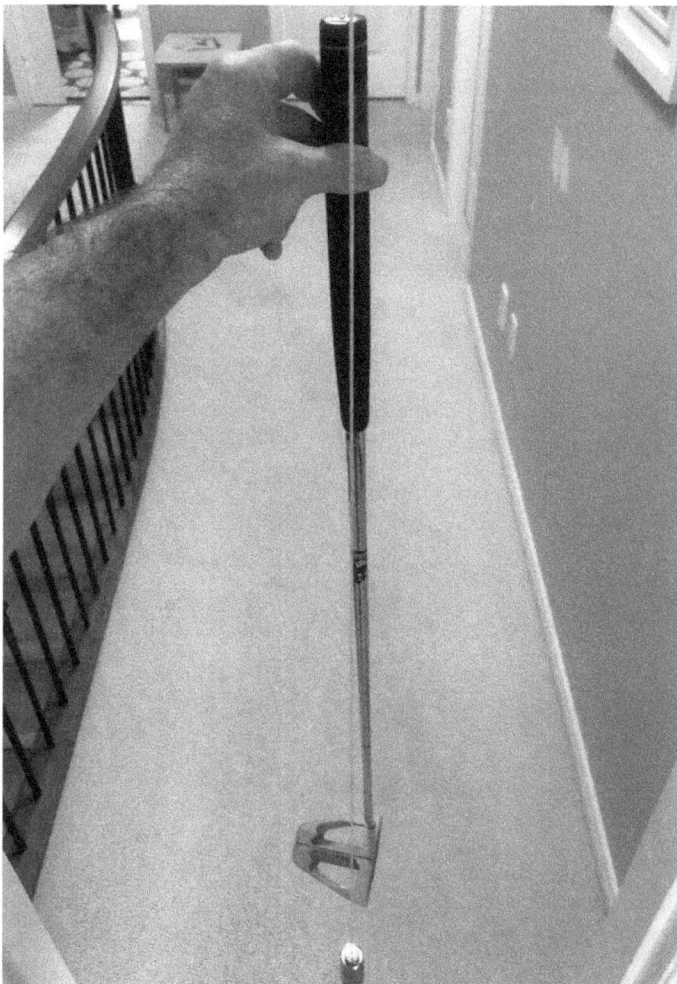

Fig. 12 Rotated Past Vertical

Once you have determined the position where your putter hangs vertically, you'll require a method to recall that position quickly and easily. Mark this vertical position in one of four ways:

Fig. 13 Mark VAP Line on Brand Sticker – For Learning ONLY

1. **Make a mental note** of the angle made by the putter head in relation to the shaft of the putter (as a key general reference). In this method, there is no mark on the putter but it is a difficult way to accurately recall the VAP while learning. It is the least repeatable legal option to use as you learn The Perfect Plumb Bob Method. And, because it will always be legal, it is listed first.

2. For the learning process only, **mark the brand manufacturer sticker with a vertical line** using a Sharpie pen (see Fig. 13 & 14) to indicate the center of the shaft location at the VAP. This step is NOT within the Rules of Golf (Rule 4.3a). If you make a mark on the brand sticker as a VAP reminder while learning The Perfect Plumb Bob Method, it must be removed (i.e., use steel wool) before playing legally on the golf course. This approach is for training purposes only.

3. Similar to 2 above, **add a strip of tape** (duct tape works well, Fig. 15) to the putter shaft and add an arrow line to make the VAP super-obvious. Note again that this tape must be removed before play (USGA Rules of Golf Rule 4.3a). Illustrations to follow (including Fig. 15) show tape with an arrow on putter shafts to remind the learner of the importance of the VAP step for all reads.

4. **Create a permanent grove line across the top of the grip handle** that defines your site line (specific reference) defining where the putter hangs in the VAP. Use a hack saw to finalize this reference by creating a shallow grove line across the butt end of the putter grip (Fig. 16 & 17). This step is within the rules of golf currently but may be somewhat controversial—and is obviously a permanent change to your putter grip. It is your best option for a permanent (and currently legal) guide to find your VAP without memorizing.

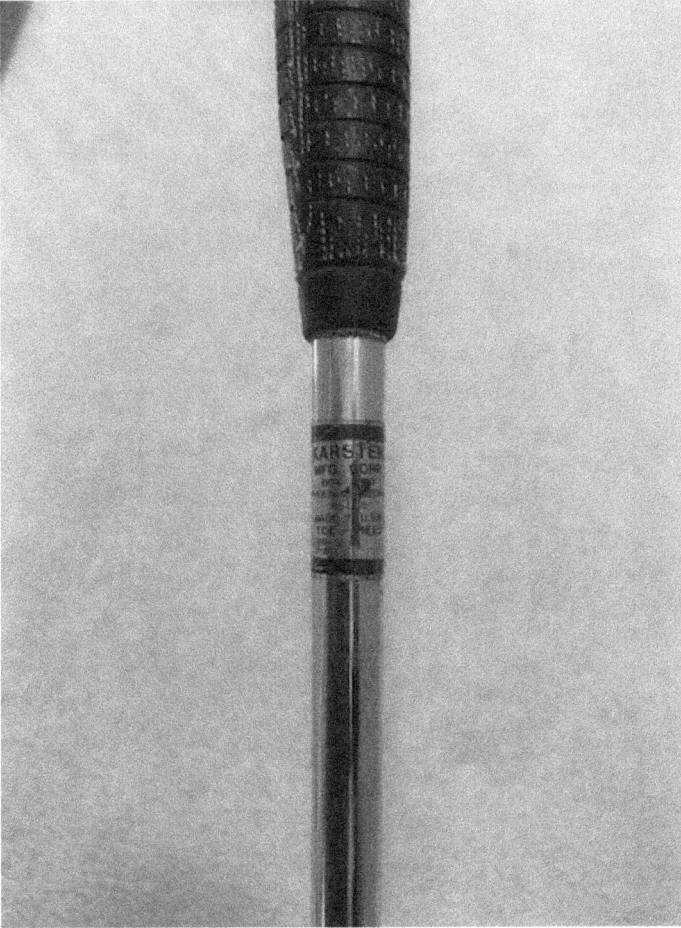

Fig 14. VAP Line on Brand Sticker – Learn ONLY

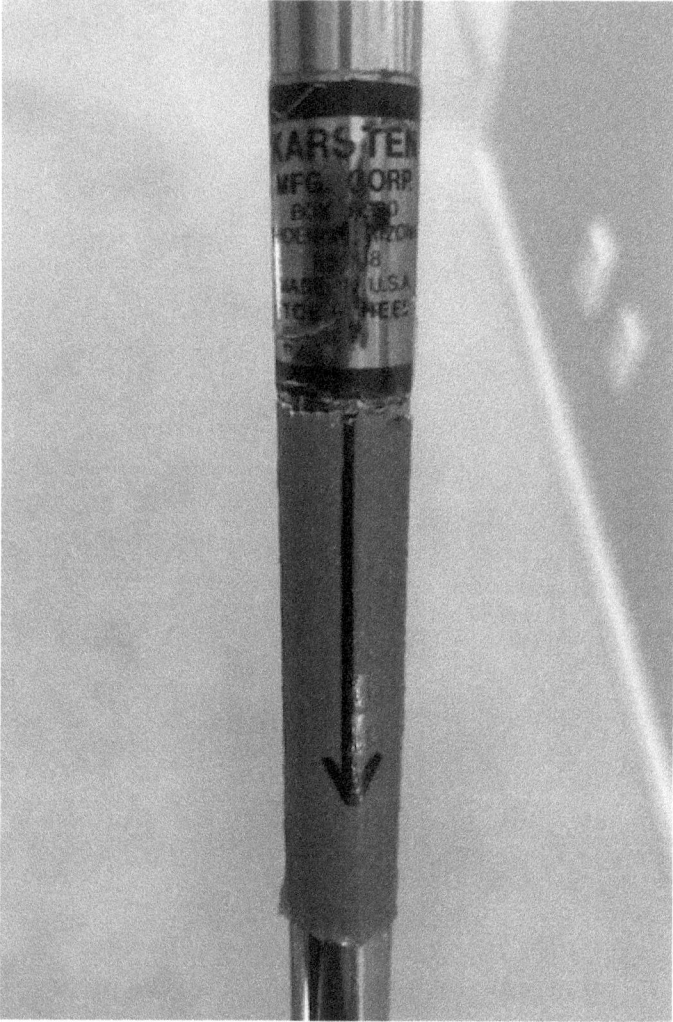

Fig. 15 VAP Arrow on Duct Tape – Learn ONLY

Fig. 16 Hack Saw Grove for VAP

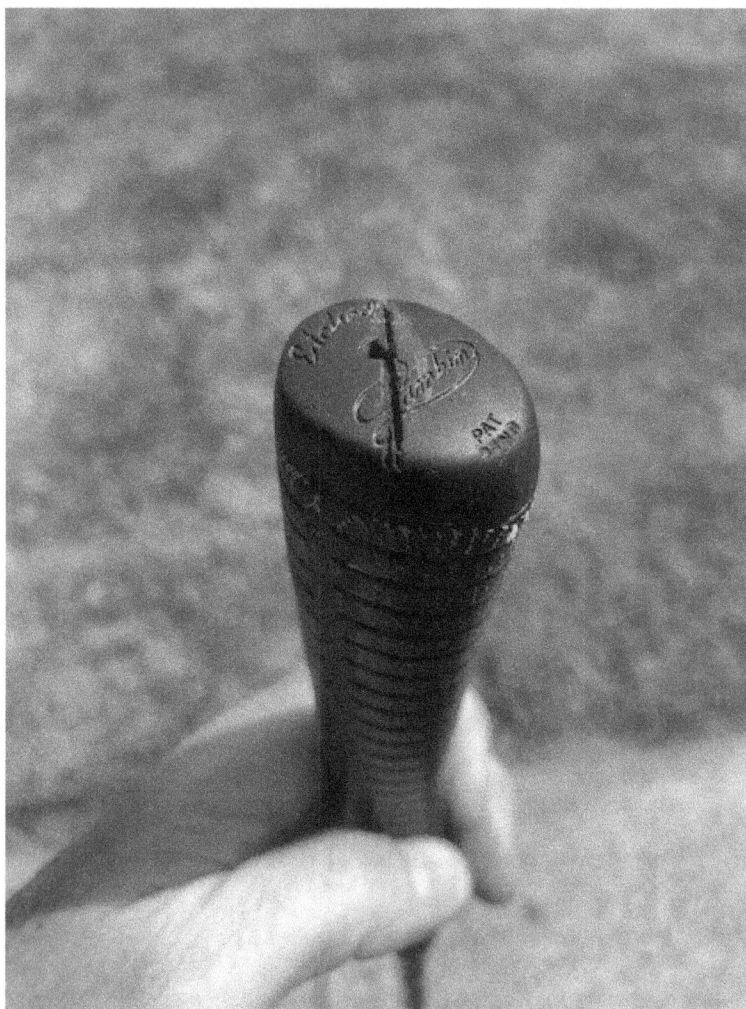

Fig. 17 Hack Saw Grove for VAP)

You now have determined the first two core tools of The Perfect Plumb Bob Method: 1) your DE and 2) your putter's VAP.

You are getting closer to being able to understand clearly what The Perfect Plumb Bob Method is about, as well as learning how valuable it can be in reading any slope. A detailed routine is essential. Another technicality is ahead that is traditionally misunderstood and omitted. This is the vital concept of '*3-Point Alignment,*' the step that positions the golfer properly to gain accurate slope information.

You are about to learn the absolute main step that foils the casual plumb bobber, *The Setup Plane (SP) & 3-Point Alignment.*

Please visit www.6footer.com to compliment the information gained within The Perfect Plumb Bob Method.

CHAPTER 3 - THE SETUP PLANE (SP) & 3-POINT ALIGNMENT

It is more than a coincidence that Chapter '3' is about '*3-Point Alignment.*' It is likely the first time most readers have heard the term '*3-Point Alignment*' which was developed by the author to create consistent body positioning for The Perfect Plumb Bob Method.

3 is a vital number in The Perfect Plumb Bob Method, especially during the initial alignment stage. This preliminary orientation step has historically been difficult to communicate to golfers when troubleshooting inconsistent plumb bobbing. *3-Point Alignment* is a phrase that works well to clear up this common misunderstanding.

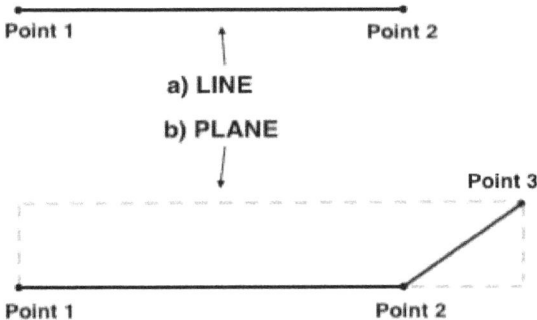

Fig. 18 Line vs. Plane

At this early stage in the book, let's pause for a simple physics discussion. *3-Point Alignment* is a core concept because The Perfect Plumb Bob Method is predicated on <u>the comparison of *a*</u>

line to *a plane.* No matter how apparently simple this may appear, *be absolutely certain that you understand the difference (See Fig. 18).*

In essence, 2 points are required to define *a line*, while 3 points are required to define a *plane* (assuming that one of the three points is not on the same line as the other two – See Fig. 18). Most golfers unknowingly compare *lines only* when plumb bobbing which creates eventual confusion.

Please get comfortable with these basic terms. We will be: a) using the concept of *3-Point Alignment* to create the **Setup *Plane* (SP)** here in Chapter 3, then b) we will create a true **Vertical *Line* (VL)** in Chapter 4, and finally c) we will learn how to compare the two (i.e., the SP vs. the VL) to read slopes and determine putt paths in Chapters 5 & 6.

So what is 3-Point Alignment in The Perfect Plumb Bob Method?

There are 3 set up points that must be properly *identified and aligned* before consistent and reliable plumb bobbing can occur.

They are as follows:

1) Your DE (Dominant Eye - Chapter 1)

2) A **Near Point (NP)**

3) A **Far Point (FP)**

Sounds simple, right?

The concept is indeed simple. It is *the delivery* of this *3-Point Alignment* step that challenges the conscious thinking of plumb bobbers new and old around the world. Getting this step *right* requires a focused commitment to comprehension, repetition, and feel. That means *practice. Yes, the 'P' word.* Over and over.

The last 2 points in *3-Point Alignment* (i.e., the Near Point (NP) and Far Point (FP)) are most often the golf ball and the hole or the hole and the golf ball, depending on what slope you are reading (though we will see in Chapter 6 that these are not the only useful points).

As noted previously, the author uses this *3-Point Alignment* perspective to set up The Perfect Plumb Bob Method because it ensures that the *newbie* (as well as the frustrated or cynical *oldie*) starts *thinking in 3's*. Mistakes or misunderstandings here are uncorrectable. Thus, you must understand it well.

Let's talk specifically now about using *3-Point Alignment* to establish your Setup Plane (SP).

3-Point Alignment (Fig. 19) is the process of aligning your DE with 2 points on the ground (i.e., a Near Point (NP) and a Far Point (FP)). Again it appears simple, but demands much repetitive feedback and learning to be consistent.

3-Point Alignment requires you to *follow* those 2 external points (i.e., the FP and NP) directly back to align with your DE.

One common stumbling point is becoming spatially aware of *where* your DE is on your body in relation to the ground. The unnatural sensation of *3-Point Alignment* becomes an innate sense only upon repeated practise and experience.

Be aware now that your Setup Plane (SP) bonds all other steps in The Perfect Plumb Bob Method. All reads and feedbacks are the result of establishing an accurate SP. Get this step right and you will become a master green reader.

It is highly advantageous to use one of the exercises below to hone in your expertise of *3-Point Alignment*:

i) Stretch a 15-20 foot string taught on the ground, on a putting green, or on an open stretch of hallway or floor indoor. Place a small object on a far point (FP) on the string. Place another small

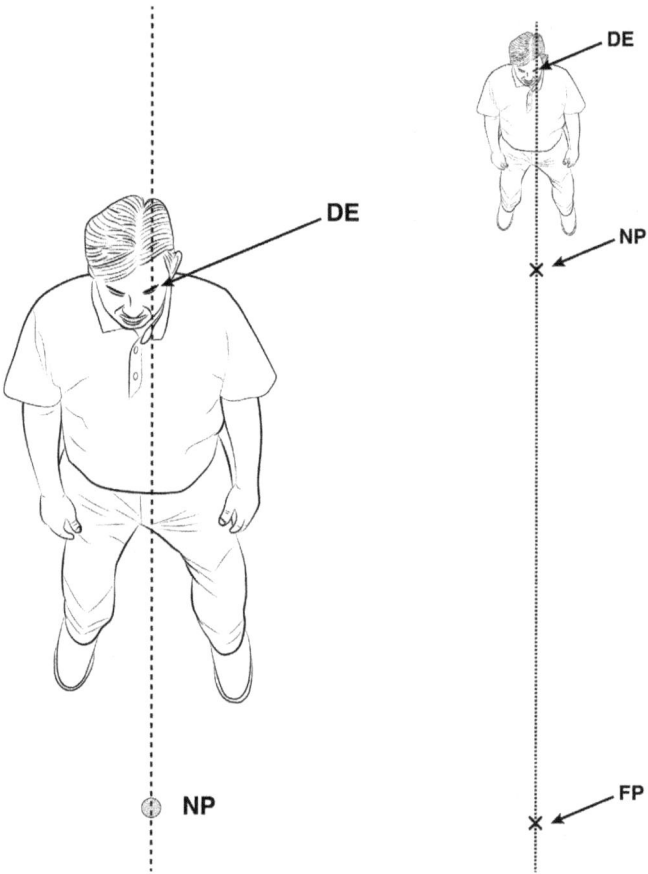

Fig. 19 3-Point Alignment (Viewed from Above)

object on a near point (NP) on the string. Position yourself at the near end of the string such that you can check to see if your DE is aligned with the string line. (See Fig. 19).

Start by ensuring consistent and healthy spinal posture. If you slouch or lean when plumb bobbing during practise or during a real round of golf, your SP will be inaccurate. Instead, shuffle your feet to move your body and DE in alignment with the FP and NP while maintaining your posture. Read this paragraph again if needed. Consistent posture is vital in setting up your SP.

Close your weak eye to activate only your DE. Gaze down by slightly flexing your neck (i.e., looking downward). Attempt to visualize where the near end of the string is relative to your DE. Shuffle your feet as discussed to align your DE with the near end of the string.

Once your DE & the string feel aligned, maintain your posture and follow the string out first to the NP, next to the FP, back again to the NP, and finally back to the near end of the string. You should feel like you are moving your head straight up and down without tilting or rotating.

If possible, have a friend or family member stand at the far end of the string and look back to give feedback as to where your DE appears relative to the string, FP and NP. Are they truly aligned?

Practise this positioning of your body until you sense your DE is being easily aligned to the string, NP and FP.

Establish a 'reference point' on your body (i.e., left or right of your sternum, navel or groin) or on the ground below you (i.e., *off-of-middle* in your stance) that you are confident is vertically below your DE. Move your head up and down such that your DE 'sees' this point in line with the string and thus the NP and FP. You will now start to get a sense of *3-Point Alignment.*

The body point or ground reference will help solidify your DE alignment. The author uses 'left of navel' as my DE reference point because I am left eye dominant.

Whisper to yourself as you proceed, for example: *'dominant eye - left of navel - near point – far point - near point - left of navel - dominant eye…* repeat and get used to this alignment mantra. The more you practise, the better you will get. You will appear to be nodding *'yes.'*

Some learners feel that it is beneficial to practise *tracing this path by pointing a finger* as you site each point. Go back and forth until you get a feel—and a clear understanding—of your own *3-Point Alignment.*

ii) Another simple way to practise *3-Point Alignment* is available if you have access to a hardwood floor or an open carpeted area that has straight lines in its pattern. As in the previous practise example, set up an NP and FP on the chosen board line or carpet line and practise aligning your DE regularly.

You will soon get a strong sense of where your DE lies in relation to the ground (or floor) below you. Remember, your DE is not in the center of your face—unless you are a Cyclopes!

Practise, practise, practise. Repeat. repeat, repeat.

In an actual golf round, you will need to be able to establish your SP instantaneously. You must become confident that your DE is in alignment with your NP and FP. It very much becomes a personal feel.

Q: To squat or to stand?

Answer: Be comfortable with both

To this point we have discussed only standing while learning The Perfect Plumb Bob Method. The author highly suggests that once you understand the initial *3-Point Alignment* process while standing, you should also repeat it while squatting. In the long term, it is beneficial to be proficient at both.

Use the same practise steps. Ensure that your spinal posture remains consistent and healthy throughout. *Again, never lean or rotate to make a read.* Always maintain an upright spine. Shuffle your feet if you must move to establish *3-Point Alignment.* It may take some additional practice to squat with control (unless you are a catcher in baseball!). It is a skill that develops through repetition. View the book cover and Fig. 19 to get a sense of the squatting posture. It is very straightforward. Always remember to be consistent.

Once you can produce *3-Point Alignment & the SP,* you have gained the main tool required to be an extremely efficient Perfect Plumb Bobber.

If there is any confusion regarding The Perfect Plumb Bob Method to this point, don't fret. Follow the process. You will have your *Ahah Moment* at some point and wonder why you haven't been plumb bobbing for a lifetime.

Your golf partners will soon think you've become a green-reading clairvoyant.

But first, let's learn how to create and integrate the true Vertical Line (VL).

CHAPTER 4 – THE VERTICAL LINE (VL)

Let's recall our brief physics lesson in Chapter 3 so that we do not become confused in understanding how The Perfect Plumb Bob Method works.

'2 points are needed to make a line. 3 points are needed to make a plane.'

The true essence and simplicity of The Perfect Plumb Bob Method boils down to *the accurate comparison of a line and a plane.*

Let's now define the fundamental line involved in The Perfect Plumb Bob Method, the true **Vertical Line (VL)**—and then let's get plumb bobbing!

We have learned in Chapter 2 how to plumb our specific putter (or putters) to a VAP (Vertical Alignment Position) such that your putter's VAP is identified using one of the suggested protocols (Reminder: If you are using a mark on the putter shaft, be sure to remove it before playing golf).

In Chapter 3, we learned the concept of *3-Point Alignment* and practiced developing an accurate Setup Plane (SP).

In Chapter 4, we will now identify 2 key points that define the true Vertical Line (VL) which in turn allow us to compare *the line to the plane* properly.

Let's be clear about the 2 points that define the true Vertical Line (VL). They are:

1) The **Lower Putter Shaft Point (LPSP)**

2) The **Upper Putter Shaft Point (UPSP)**

Where the slope of the green is nil (i.e., the green is flat), the true Vertical Line (VL) will blend exactly over the Setup Plane (SP). Note that short game guru, Dave Pelz, points out that '98% of our putts are breaking because architects have to build them that way for drainage.'

Thus, don't expect to see a lot of perfectly flat reads, but they are helpful to illustrate the contrast between flat and sloped ground. A flat vs. sloped ground comparison (Fig. 20) helps to differentiate the VL points from the SP points for clarity.

Let's break down these 2 points of the VL to gain a clear understanding of what they are—and what their uses are—in The Perfect Plumb Bob Method.

1. Lower Putter Shaft Point (LPSP) – Determine the LPSP by hovering your vertically plumbed putter (VAP from Chapter 2) such that the NP (Chapter 3) is covered by <u>an arbitrary point that you select</u> on the lower portion of the putter shaft. This point becomes your LPSP for your current plumb bob effort.

When hovering your putter, hold the putter gently near the top of the grip by pinching lightly with your thumb and index or middle finger, whichever is more comfortable. Hold the putter at the same location on the grip each time (Chapter 2). The putter should hang freely with gravity.

The LPSP is not a specific location on the putter shaft and may be slightly different for every plumb bob read. It can be any point on the lower portion of the putter shaft, but lower is better because of putter shaft design.

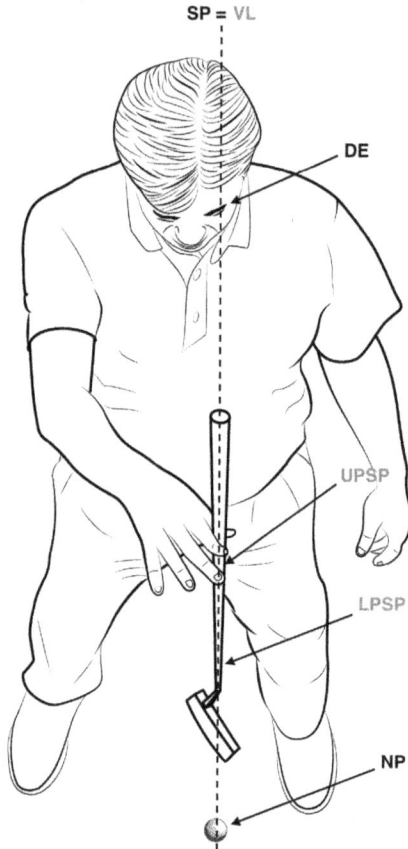

Fig. 20 Nil slope, VL = SP (Standing, Viewed from Above)

Most putter shafts are tapered, meaning that the shaft widens moving from the putter head end up to the grip handle end. This factor will eventually pose an inconvenience for plumb bobbers, especially when reading subtle slopes.

More on this subject later in the book, including a helpful shortcut solution.

For now, get in the habit of choosing an arbitrary LPSP that is low on the putter shaft.

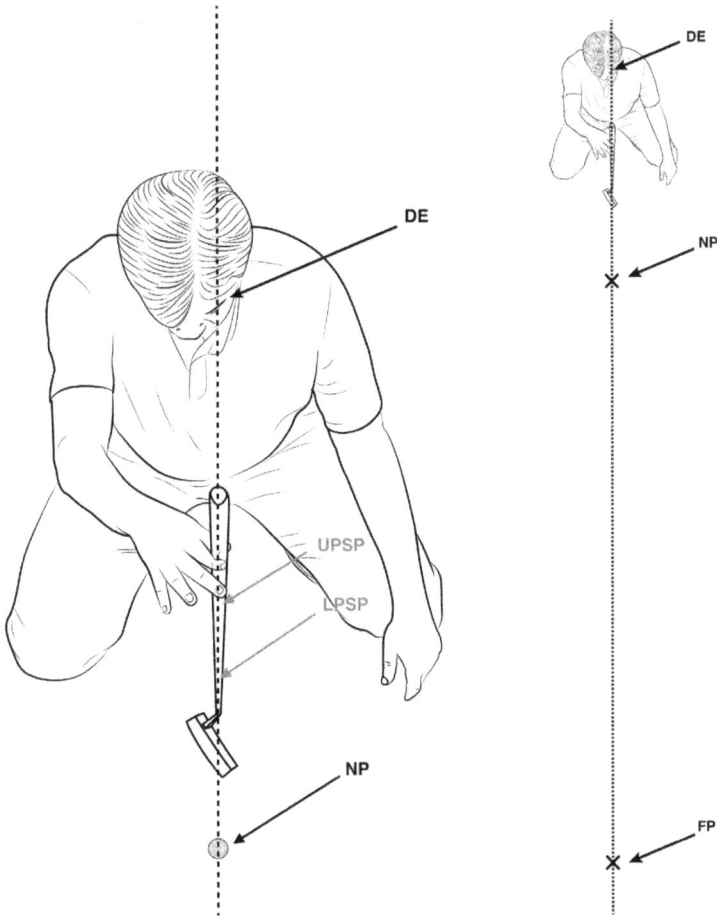

Fig. 21 Nil Slope, VL = SP (Squatting, Viewed from Above)

On perfectly level ground, the VL and the SP blend together (Fig. 20) and the DE, UPSP, LPSP, NP & FP are all on the same plane.

2. Upper Putter Shaft Point (UPSP) - Let's be careful to avoid confusion while visualizing the UPSP, as we are close to tying all chapters together thus far. For now,

understand that the UPSP will be a point on the upper part of the vertically plumb putter shaft that is <u>level in the sight line</u> with the Far Point (FP) from Chapter 3.

When the slope below the plumb bobber is nil (i.e., the ground is level) the UPSP will cover the FP.

If this detail seems confusing, worry not. Simply know that the level of the UPSP is determined secondarily by the sight level of the FP. **The UPSP is the variable that will help us detect slope (i.e., *which way?* and *how much?*) in The Perfect Plumb Bob Method.**

Clear? Confused? Fear not, because in Chapter 5 we will compare the VL and the SP and start to tie the whole method together.

It's time to read some putts.

CHAPTER 5 – COMPARING THE SP & VL: READING PUTTS!

You've made it well to this point. Let's now put it all together and delve into the real-world golf applications of The Perfect Plumb Bob Method.

Proper plumb bobbing will be well defined after this chapter— and after a good bit of practise.

First, a quick recap of The Perfect Plumb Bob Method thus far. Better to spend a bit of focused time now to solidify our knowledge than to struggle later in frustration.

We determined our DE in Chapter 1.

We determined the VAP of our putter in Chapter 2.

We used *3-Point Alignment* to congeal our SP in Chapter 3.

We determined the 2 useful points—the LPSP and UPSP—that define our true vertical line (VL) in Chapter 4.

In Chapter 5, we begin to apply all and learn what happens when the SP and VL do not match—*which is most of the time*. We now learn 1) how to read ground slope and 2) how to use that information to read greens—and *to make a ton of putts*.

As mentioned earlier, body position during plumb bobbing can be standing or squatting. In either stance, spinal posture must remain consistent while setting up each SP. Feet should be shoulder width apart when standing (unless otherwise instructed)

43

and under the butt bones (i.e., ischial tuberosities) when squatting.

One strong warning: Do not delay play. Learn to be an efficient Perfect Plumb Bobber and to be respectful of other players.

The boring part is over. Let's first consider the variables involved when our SP and VL do not match. Once understood, the only activity left is reading greens! Here we go.

Refer to Fig. 22 and Fig. 23 to observe first that when the ground under foot is sloped, the VL and SP no longer match. Notice that the crossing point of the VL and the SP is at the LPSP (circled). In The Perfect Plumb Bob Method, this will always be the reference point from which all 'line & plane (i.e., VL & SP)' comparisons ultimately originate.

In other words, the LPSP will always appear to be on both the VL and the SP.

Study these figures and be sure to understand this *line vs. plane* comparison thoroughly. Notice specifically that when a surface is sloped, *the UPSP moves off of the SP*, indicating that the golfer's body has settled onto the *low side* of the sloped surface.

Both the mystery and the clarity can now begin to take shape.

*a) **Reading Ball-Side Slope** – The First Factor in Reading Putt Break*

Refer to Fig. 24 and have your first look at a mockup view of a golfer's site line while using The Perfect Plumb Bob Method. Here is where we begin to put all details of all previous steps together into functional action.

The putter hangs vertically plumb (VAP) as the golfer hovers the putter shaft such that the LPSP covers the NP, in this case the golf ball.

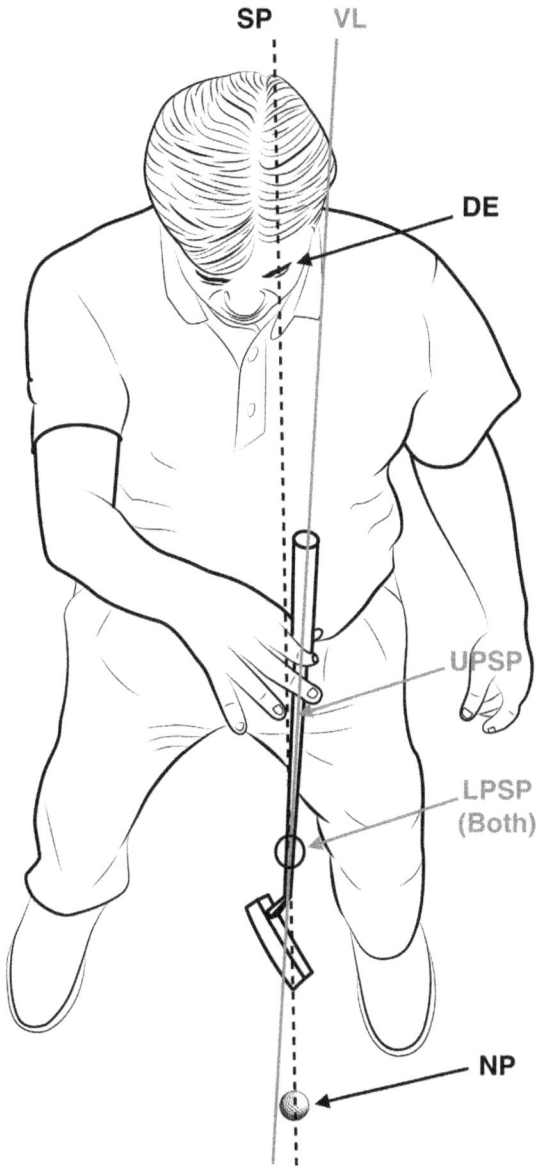

Fig. 22 SP vs. VL - Slope (Standing, Viewed from Above)

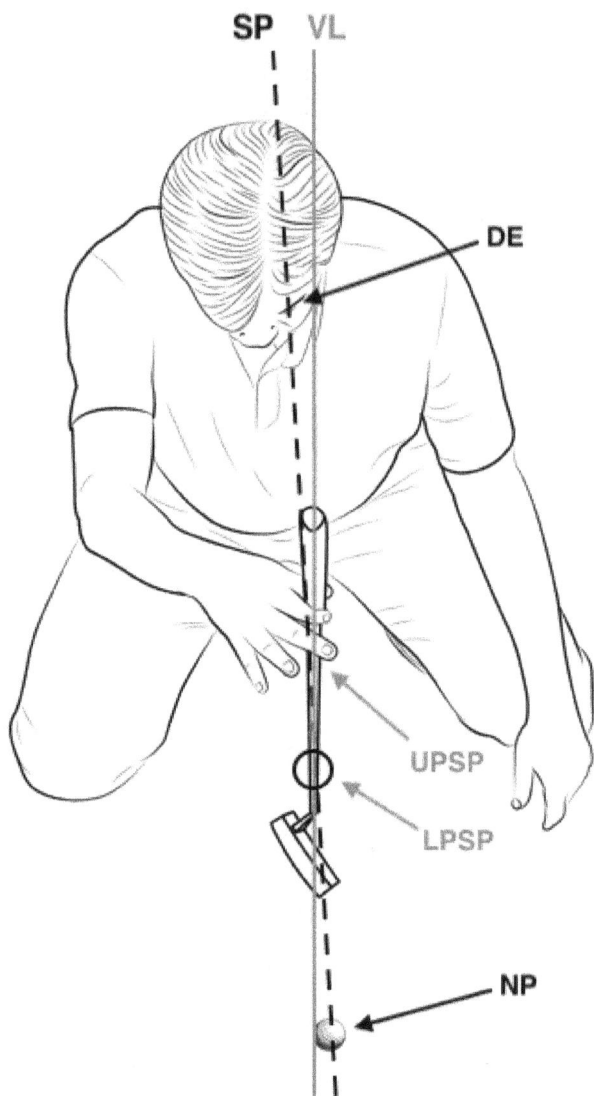

Fig. 23 SP vs. VL - Slope (Squatting, Viewed from Above)

The golfer is now able to compare the FP (the hole, in this case) from the SP with the UPSP from the VL (reread as needed!).

Q: Where is the FP located relative the UPSP in Fig. 24?
A: *To the left.*

In other words, the golfer's body (including DE) has **settled *to the left*** of true **vertical**, indicating that the surface below the golfer **slopes *to the left*.**

PPB RULE #1

The side to which the FP deviates away from the VL indicates the ***direction of the slope***.

PPB RULE #2

The distance that the FP deviates away from the VL indicates the ***severity of the slope.***

All tedious preparation using The Perfect Plumb Bob Method now gives instant feedback regarding ground slope—and the proper path of the putt.

But wait—there is more to understand. Much more.

Many plumb bob efforts stop here after gaining some sense of control of putt path dynamics. It is another stumbling point that will eventually lead to frustration, myth and abandonment.

The Perfect Plumb Bob Method is well under way. If you have been deliberate in absorbing all particulars presented thus far, you have already gained a deep understanding of discovering slope. You are doing well. You have developed most of the basic skills needed to plumb bob properly—and efficiently.

What you must now understand is the proper *application* of these skills. The reader must *learn what is being learned* about slope

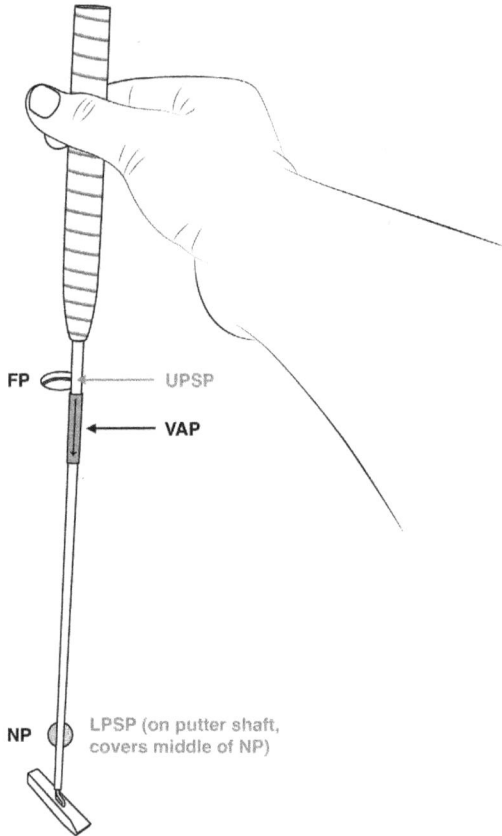

Fig. 24 Ball-Side Slope (R-L slight)

and comprehend how to apply the feedback appropriately to maximize putting success—and to recognize limitations.

From this point on you become a serious Perfect Plumb Bobber and a clairvoyant green reader.

A most misunderstood question to start with: *What slope am I reading?*

Let's now recall that we create the SP via proper application of

3-Point Alignment. The 3 points are: the DE, the NP, and the FP. The position of the NP and FP are inarguably static. It is the DE that requires further discussion.

The location of the DE is *the factor* that will tilt (or not tilt) the SP away from the VL. If the ground is level below the golfer, the golfer's body, DE and SP remain on the VL. If the ground is sloped, the golfer's body, DE and SP will settle off of the VL.

Thus, all users of The Perfect Plumb Bob Method must realize clearly that slope information gained is ONLY in relation to *the surface below the golfer.* This is a vital fundamental that must be *completely understood* if slope information gained is to be properly applied.

See Fig. 25. Be clear, it is ground slope in the shaded area below the golfer that gives all feedback.

The good news is that most golf greens are smooth in slope and design. Golfers can extrapolate the slope below them to be the same as (or similar to) the green surface around them.

If the area of the green being read does have an extreme slope change, such as a hill or hollow, it will be obvious to the naked eye and will not require further detection.

Thus, putts that have a single slope (i.e., right to left (R-L) or left to right (L-R)) are much easier to read and plan than longer or multiple breaking putts which require assimilation of multiple slopes at multiple locations.

The point is, first be aware of the true slope you are reading. Only then can you consider *how* that slope affects the entire path of your putt. Know your limitations.

The Perfect Plumb Bob Method refers to *'Perfect'* in regard to the set up and, ultimately, the routine. It is never intended to infer that the information gained is indicative of any *absolutes* or

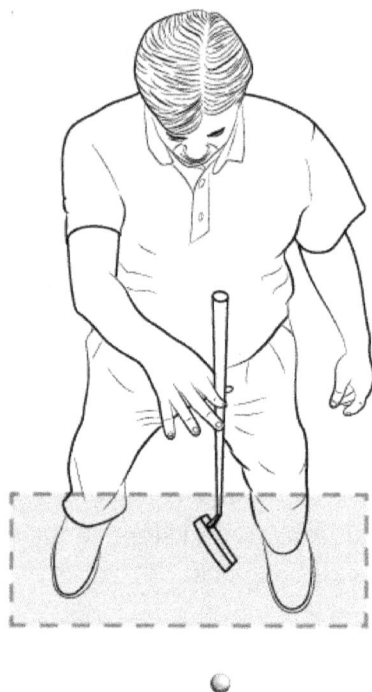

Fig. 25 What Slope Am I Reading?

perfect quantitative measurements.

The goal of The Perfect Plumb Bob Method is to gain valuable and dependable slope feedback that the Perfect Plumb Bobber may then utilize to their best advantage in determining a confident putt path that leads *directly* to more made putts.

Let's study more *ball-side* slope reads and advance our skills in *seeing slope*.

Fig. 26 and 27 represent two more Perfect Plumb Bob examples from the ball-side of the putt.

Fig. 26 represents the rare straight putt read. This is what the golfer will witness when the ground below her or him is level. The SP and VL are the same.

Fig. 27 represents an extreme left to right (L-R) slope to begin the putt. Note that the FP (i.e. the hole) is further away from the UPSP than represented in Fig. 24. Thus, the slope is greater.

Reminder 1: The side that the FP deviates away from the VL (UPSP) indicates *the direction of the slope.*

Reminder 2: The distance that the FP deviates away from the VL (UPSP) indicates *the severity of the slope.*

The information gained is qualitative, not quantitative, giving us a vital *sense* of our putt path.

Make sense to this point? Let's move more deeply and advance greatly as a Perfect Plumb Bobber and ask the next profound putting question...

What slope lends the most to the putt path—the slope at the start of the putt or the slope at the end?

The answer is: ***both.***

The ball generally carries most of its speed at the start of the putt. Thus, it can be tempting to conclude that the starting slope is not *the most* important factor in reading the putt (i.e., the ball is moving *too fast to break*) or may even be *unimportant*, especially regarding longer or multi-breaking putts.

But the starting slope of the putt *is a key factor* to all putt paths because it sets the ***initial directional momentum*** for the entire putt. On shorter putts, it will tell you *a lot* or all of the proper putt path story. On longer and multi-breaking putts, the starting slope sets the ball in motion on its initial direction.

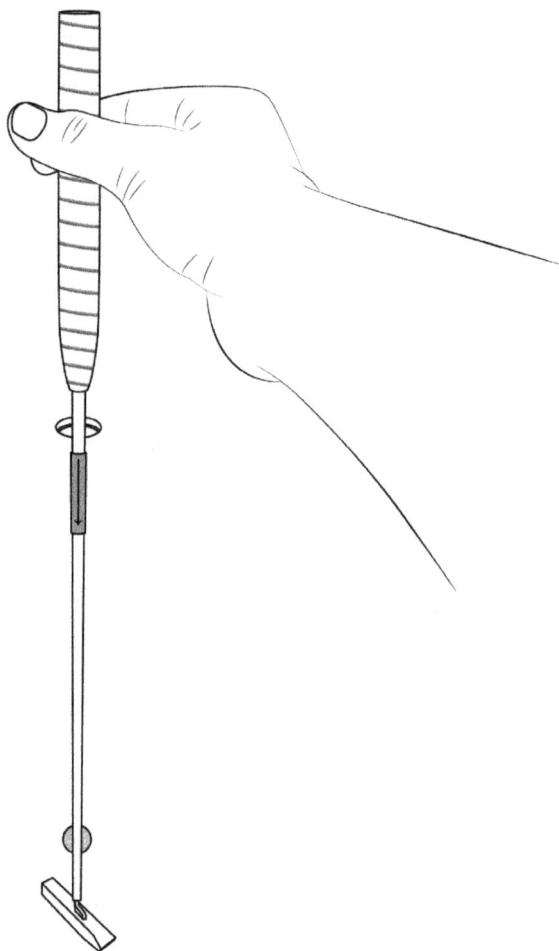

Fig. 26 Ball-Side Slope (Level)

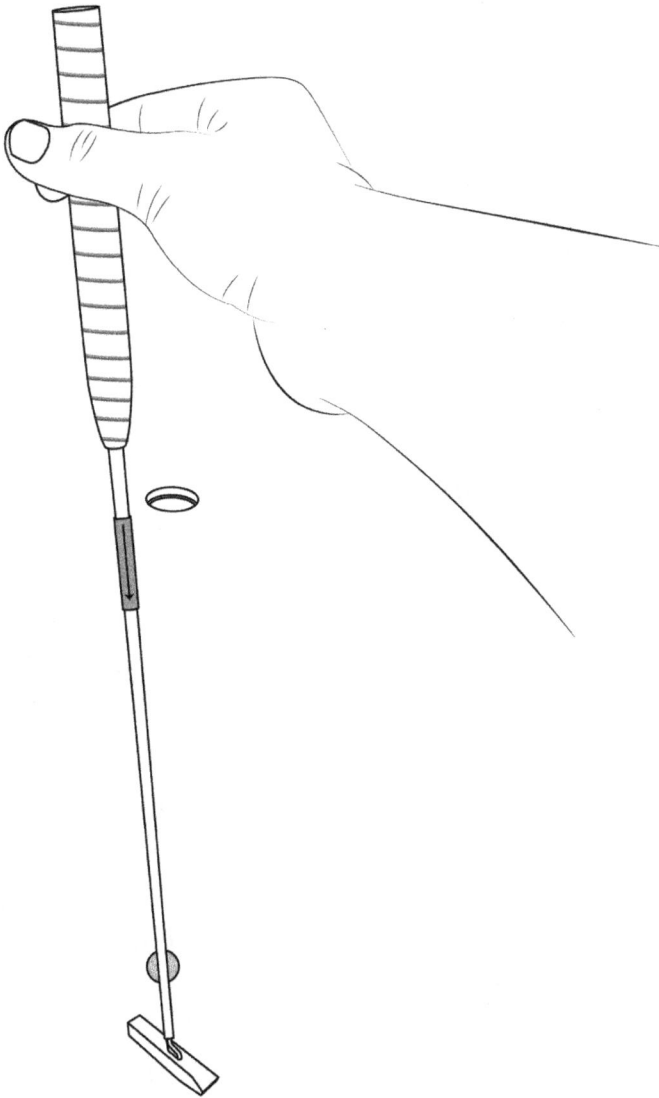

Fig. 27 Ball-Side Slope (Extreme L-R)

We know from physics and Newton's First Law of Motion (The Law of Inertia) that *an object in motion tends to stay in motion unless acted upon by an outside force.* This is true for the starting slope of each putt.

The initial momentum of the golf ball continues until acted on by the frictional forces of grass and slope along the rest of the putt. It is vital to know the starting slope of each putt because we must know the initial directional momentum for that putt.

That said, putts *do* break *more* as they run out of speed. Thus, we must *also* gain vital information regarding the slope of the ground at the end of the putt. The end slope tells us *how the putt will finish.*

b) Reading Hole-Side Slope – *The Second Factor in Reading Putt Break*

Let's now travel to the hole-side of the putt, reverse the FP and NP, and use The Perfect Plumb Bob Method to accrue slope information from the *end of the putt*, when the putt loses speed and may break a lot.

Fig. 28 offers our first look at viewing slope from the hole-side. It's time to *see what the hole sees.* The hole is now the NP, the ball the FP.

Where the <u>ball-side read</u> is vital to determine *initial putt momentum*, <u>the hole-side</u> read exposes the *final putt finish.* As mentioned, because the ball as it is slowing in speed, the final slope has a great influence on the putt path.

The basic mechanics of The Perfect Plumb Bob Method read remain unchanged, but a not-so-subtle adjustment is required mentally regarding the golfer's ***putt path perspective***.

The *putt path perspective* used in The Perfect Plumb Bob Method will always be referenced from a *ball-to-hole orientation.*

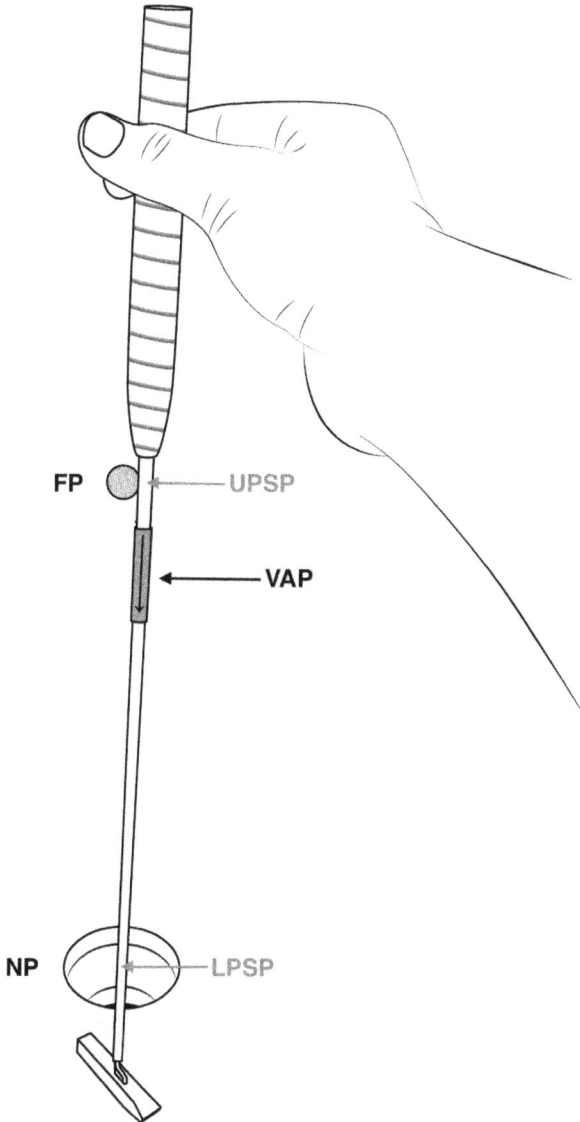

Fig. 28 Hole-Side Slope (L-R Small)

If one looks at Fig. 28 for example, one sees that the slope from behind the hole is to the left—but the stated ball break is slightly left to right. This may be confusing to the newbie Perfect Plumb Bobber because—though we are viewing the final slope of the putt *from the hole-side*—we are still referring to the putt break pattern from a *ball-to-hole orientation*.

To avoid confusion, just remember that no matter what end of the putt we are reading a putt from (i.e., ball-side or hole-side), we are always assimilating our final putt path from a *ball-to-hole orientation*.

Look again at Fig. 28. The slope is to the left (when viewed from behind the hole). The break at the end of the putt is slightly left to right (from a *ball-to-hole orientation*).

Mental statement: 'The putt will finish slightly to the right.'

Read these last few paragraphs as necessary. They are all simply explaining the necessity to keep in mind that we organize our complete putt path plan from a *ball-to-hole orientation*. It is a matter of semantics and must remain organized and consistent.

Many examples will follow that will train and solidify the reader's thinking, analyzing, and final mental putt planning.

Let's become aware of another factor that requires understanding in The Perfect Plumb Bob Method. Fig. 29 illustrates the principle of a *divergent FP appearance*. The FP will appear to deviate more from the UPSP when the FP is further in the distance, even though the slope below the golfer remains unchanged.

The example in Fig. 29 uses 1 golf ball to represent a NP and additional golf balls to represent 5 distant FPs that are spaced equally apart. Though all 5 sample FPs are located on the same plane on the SP, they appear to deviate more from the VL (i.e.,

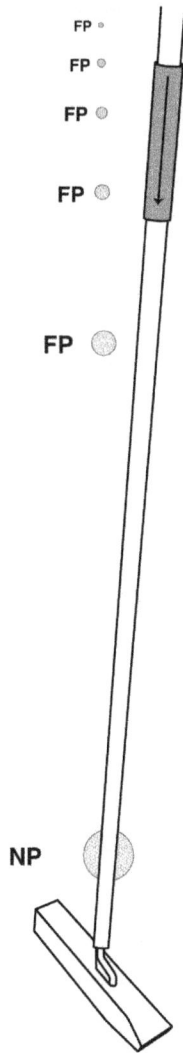

FP ·
FP ◦
FP ○
FP ◉
FP ◉

NP

Fig. 29 Divergent FP Appearance

from the UPSP) as they are farther away, yet the slope illustrated is no different.

Thus, there will always be the *appearance* of greater slope as the FP is further away from the NP. Experience alone will allow The Perfect Plumb Bobber to best assimilate this distance illusion factor. Please be aware of it now.

The distance between the FP and the UPSP will never correlate to a measureable amount of break (i.e., 1" between FP and UPSP does not mean x feet of break). Instead, it correlates to qualitative information pertaining to the ground below the golfer: the slope is left, right or level and is slight, moderate, extreme or somewhere in between.

That is not to say that The Perfect Plumb Bob Method is not specific. Indeed, it reveals real and direct feedback which becomes more specific with practice. The information gained becomes a key ingredient within an entire putt reading process.

Now that we understand *the process* and *the slope* that is being read, let's dig even deeper.

It's time to see the full power of The Perfect Plumb Bob Method at work and learn about its many applications. It's time to turn the lights on fully.

For example, there are not just 2 reads (i.e., *ball-side* and *hole-side*), as most plumb bobbers believe...

There are 7!

CHAPTER 6 - THE 7 READS

In Chapter 5, we learned how to compare the SP with the VL to get our first taste of reading slope using The Perfect Plumb Bob Method.

Let's keep the learning going. The rest of the reads are based on the same principles. You have gained the ability to read any surface to gain any slope information. Let me explain...

Thus far, we have had 3 points predetermined for our 3-Point Alignment process. These 3 points may have originally seemed difficult to align due to unfamiliarity. Through practice, *3-Point Alignment* has made it possible and then practical to compare your accurate SP to a VL.

Now consider: What if you only had 2 points of reference with which to create your SP? A pronounced benefit of becoming proficient with *3-Point Alignment* is that you will now be able to create an SP with only 2 points, as well as with only 1 point.

Seem like a stretch? I assure you, The Perfect Plumb Bob Method opens up the world of slope reading to those who commit to the process.

Now you can learn each of 7 important reads that may be asked of you in any green-reading or slope-reading situation. Learn them well and add them to your tool kit. You are about to advance quickly as a green reader, and in turn as a putter and a scorer in golf.

Read #1: Ball-Side Break

Ball-side break was covered in Chapter 5. A quick review of the pertinent points:

a) The slope being read is below the golfer,
b) The ball-side break gives us information on the start of the putt and thus on the initial directional momentum of the putt.

Read #2: Hole-Side Break

Hole-side break was also covered in Chapter 5. A quick review:

a) The slope being read is below the golfer,
b) The hole-side break gives us information pertaining to the end of the putt and thus the final finishing path of the putt, where the putt will lose speed and tend to break more,
c) Reminder: the mental putt read is always categorized from a *ball-to-hole* reference.

Read #3: Mid-Putt Break (Multi-Breaking Putt)

The mid-putt read is utilized to gain information about the midway slope of a putt and is useful when a golfer is reading a multi-break putt.

Which part of the putt has more effect on the net outcome of the putt path, the starting break or the finishing break? Where does the break change? These are the questions answered by the mid-putt read.

To perform the mid-putt read, the golfer must <u>straddle</u> the putt line at whatever point in the putt the read is desired. Notice that the NP (i.e., the golf ball) is missing in a mid-putt read (See Fig. 30). To make this read, The Perfect Plumb Bobber must improvise an NP (i.e., find a spot, mark, or imperfection on the green) that is easily recognized and in alignment with the two other *3-Point Alignment* variables (i.e., DE and FP).

On most golf courses, a spot, mark or imperfection is easy to find as your new NP.

Upon practise, you will soon find that setting up creative SP's becomes virtually innate. This read and others will soon become clear and simple. Several reads to follow demand an improvised NP or FP or both.

The feedback gained from a mid-putt read can be synthesized with the rest of your green reading information to devise an accurate and decisive putt path plan.

Read #4: Ball-Side Speed

Let's peel off another layer of uncertainty in our ability to develop concise putt plans by adding a unique category of Perfect Plumb Bob reads: *Putt speed.*

The Perfect Plumb Bob Method delivers several strategies for realizing slope feedback related to the speed of any putt. Let's discuss the *ball-side speed* first.

Refer to Fig. 31a to understand the body position required to read the specific slope that affects the initial speed of any putt. In this read, your SP (and thus your body) is positioned perpendicular to the line of your putt.

Always take into consideration the putt paths of your playing partners and note that you may stand perpendicular to your putt line on either side, whichever is clear and most convenient.

Your golf ball is now your NP, and your FP will have to be improvised. Find an FP that is on your SP in line with your DE and NP. Reread as needed.

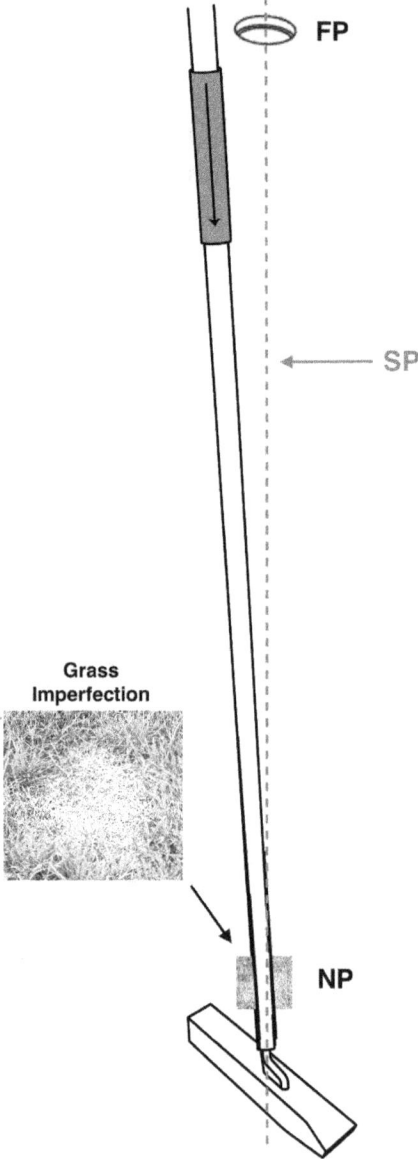

Fig. 30 Mid-Putt Break (Straddling Putt Line)

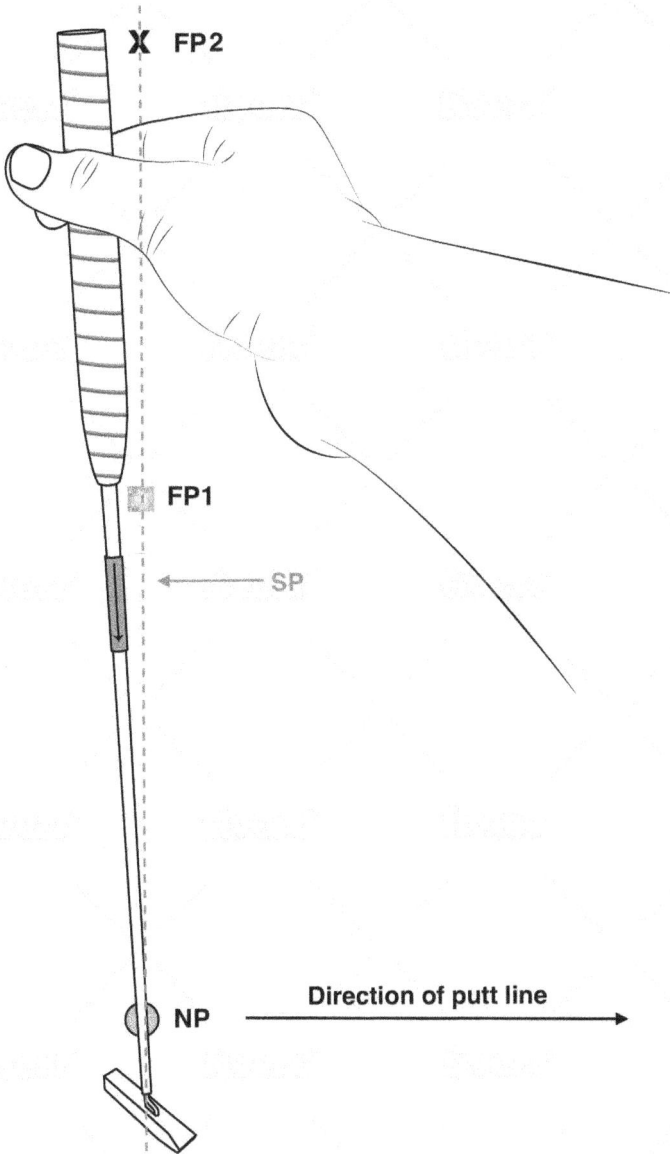

Fig. 31a Ball-Side Speed (SP Perpendicular to Putt Line)

Here's how: Look for either: a) a nearby a spot, mark, or imperfection on the green beyond the NP (See FP1 in Fig. 31a),

63

or alternatively b) an object or marker well in the distance (i.e., a bush, sprinkler head, golf bag, etc.) that is aligned on the SP (See FP2 in Fig. 31a).

This statement may sound confusing on first perusal, but it is not difficult. There is always a mark (near or in the distance) that catches one's eye beyond the NP, along the SP. The key to reading the *ball-side speed* rests on your ability to create an SP that is perpendicular to your putt line. Practise will make this process quick and automatic.

Thus, in Fig. 31a, can you conclude the slope to start this putt?

The initial slope of the putt is downhill because the FP (1 or 2) has deviated to the right of the UPSP. The slope is to the right in the direction of the putt line.

Remember that you are technically reading the slope *directly below your feet*. Speed reads, as all others reads, are extrapolations.

Stand close and perpendicular to the ball (assuming that no other player's putt paths are affected) to minimize this extrapolation. If your putt has vast variations in slope nearby that may challenge this extrapolation of speed (i.e., a hump or hill), the speed would be obvious and not require this type of read.

Read #5: Hole-Side Speed

Once you become confident with the adjustments required to read *ball-side speed* using The Perfect Plumb Bob Method, reading *hole-side speed* becomes straightforward and easily applicable.

To exercise the reader's mind, let's look at a *hole-side speed* scenario just the same.

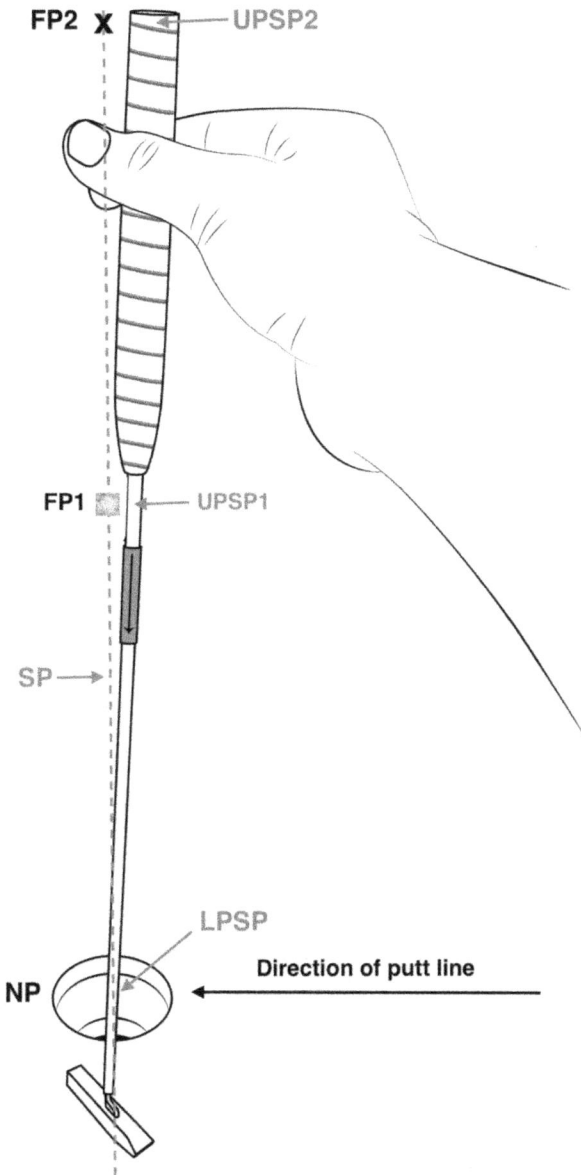

FP2 X ——UPSP2

FP1 ——UPSP1

SP——

LPSP

NP

Direction of putt line

Fig. 31b Hole-Side Speed (SP Perpendicular to Putt Line)

Observe Fig. 31b and note that the golfer is once again positioned such that their SP is set up perpendicular to the line of the putt. Either side of the hole is acceptable—whichever is most convenient— always respecting the putt paths of fellow players.

Notice that the NP is now the center of the hole. FP1 option is a spot, mark, or imperfection on the green (see Fig. 31b) beyond the NP along the SP, or FP2 option (see the X in Fig. 31b) is any object (i.e. a bush, sprinkler head, golf bag, etc.) in the distance along the SP.

Whichever FP catches your eye first completes the *3-Point Alignment.*

Again, on first perusal this explanation may sound complicated or difficult to complete. With practise, improvising an FP will become simple and automatic.

Q: In the scenario in Fig. 31, is the speed at the end of this putt uphill, downhill or level?

A: It is downhill because the FP (i.e., either FP1 or FP2) deviates to the left of the sample UPSP, and thus the slope is to the left. Because the putt line is from the right, this putt has a moderate downhill finish.

Read #6: Mid-Putt Speed

We've looked at how to read slope for ball-side speed and we've looked at how to read slope for hole-side speed. Now let's consider situations where we may want to clarify the speed of a putt at $\frac{1}{3}$, $\frac{1}{2}$, or $\frac{3}{4}$ of the way, or at any point throughout the putt.

How do we use The Perfect Plumb Bob Method to read the mid-putt speed, if needed? Upon understanding Reads #4 and #5, this read is more forthright, and can give us valuable information in very specific circumstances.

For example, see Fig. 32. On long putts, there may exist a downhill and/or uphill component that is difficult to see (or sense) with the naked eye. Just as in a multi-breaking putt, it may be helpful to know what is happening speed-wise at any point along the putt path. For example, how much of the putt path is uphill? How much is downhill? Where does the speed change?

Position yourself perpendicular the putt line at the point where you are questioning the speed of the putt. Again, be respectful of the putt paths of fellow players.

In reading mid-putt speed, you will have to improvise *both an NP and an FP* in the process of setting up the SP that is perpendicular to the putt path.

Mentally create an SP line that is perpendicular to your putt path and improvise a near spot, mark, or imperfection on the green to act as the NP on that line. Next improvise an FP that is the distance and along your SP to complete your *3-Point Alignment.*

Hover your putter such that the LPSP covers the NP. Observe the FP in relation to the UPSP. In Fig. 32, the mid-putt slope is to the right, revealing an uphill mid-putt slope. The putt is slow in the middle.

Improvising both the NP and the FP may seem like a daunting task to the beginner, but it is not difficult. With practise and experience, your ability to create a perpendicular SP's will quickly improve to a point where it is easy, automatic and dependable.

Read #7: The Straight Putt Line

Read #7 takes us into the final stage of the basic reads of The Perfect Plumb Bob Method. I'll show you two ways to determine the *straight putt line,* or what is commonly called the *fault line.*

The author also refers to this line as *The Jet Stream Line* for

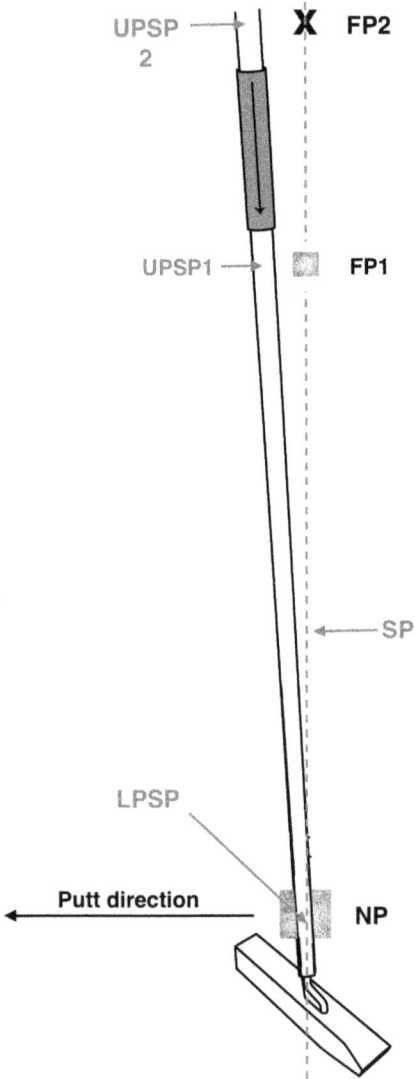

Fig. 32 Mid-Putt Speed (SP Perpendicular to Putt Line)

reasons discussed later in this chapter. It can be an important reference line for reading final break of any putt, but is used almost exclusively in reference to shorter putts (i.e., six feet and in).

What is the straight putt line?

The straight putt line is that line where, whether a ball is above (downhill putt) or below the hole (uphill putt), the putt will run straight. It is a useful line to find and know on a big-sloped green area.

The straight putt line is important to identify because it divides the break pattern. An uphill putt from the left of the line will break left to right (L-to-R) and from the right of the line will break right to left (R-to-L). The same rule applies for a downhill putt perspective.

Knowing the straight putt line helps golfers become more proficient and precise putt readers (See Fig. 33), especially on short putts on sloped greens. The more your ball deviates from the straight putt line, the more the putt will break.

When you know where the straight putt line is, you become very aware of putts that can *get away from you* and break sharply. You can virtually eliminate the *surprise factor* that brings the strangest (and you may soon find, *the most entertaining*) expressions to the faces of golfers as their putt *just snaps!*

Finding *the straight putt line* requires a quick trial and error effort using The Perfect Plumb Bob Method.

(See Fig. 34) First, make your best guess at where the straight putt line may be located (i.e., what putt line *looks* straight?). Next, create your *3-Point Alignment* on that line using your DE, the center of the hole as your NP, and improvise an FP beyond the hole along your guessed SP.

Now compare your VL to your SP. Does your FP deviate from your UPSP? Or are they in alignment? If they are in alignment, you have found your *straight putt line.*

If not, be aware that if you have found a right slope (as in Fig. 34 (a)), the straight putt line will be to your right (vice versa for a left slope). Move to your right and test a new SP until the FP and UPSP overlap (see Fig. 34 (b)).

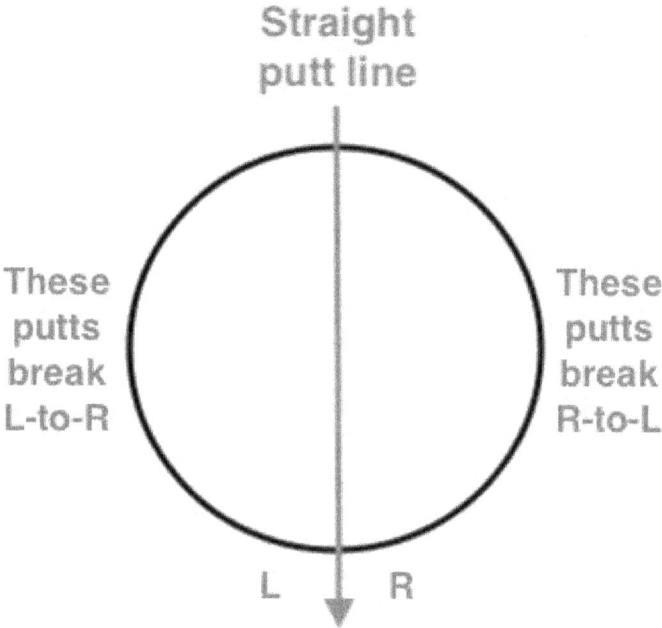

Straight putt line

These putts break L-to-R

These putts break R-to-L

L   R

Fig. 33 Straight Putt Line (Uphill Putt)

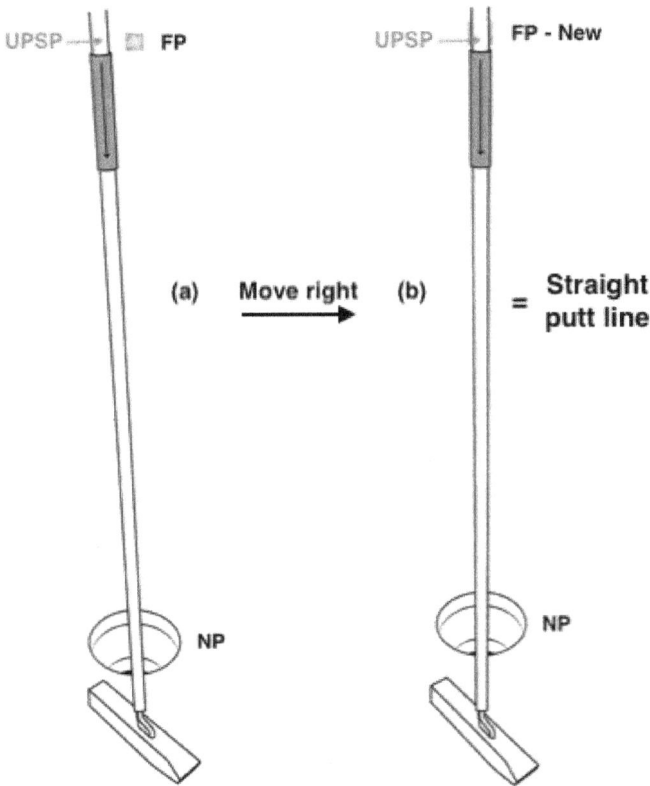

Fig. 34 Straight Putt Line Search

When you become a proficient Perfect Plumb Bobber, finding this line will not take long and will give the golfer strong feedback regarding how much their putt will break. It is most useful and accurate on big sloped green areas, and thus should be used as a check tool.

Tip: **See the *straight putt line* as *The Jet Stream Line***

There is more to the *straight putt line* than first meets the eye. *It* is not just a static line. *It* affects the break of putts (especially on big slopes) and is to be respected. *It* is a factor within why most people under-read putts.

71

For these reasons, the author refers to this line as *'The Jet Stream Line,'* especially when a putt is down-slope and down-grain (i.e., the grain of the grass runs in the same direction as the putt path).

Here's why…

The Jet Stream Line represents the highest point on the cup (on the high side) and the lowest point on the cup (on the low side).

It sounds counter-intuitive to state, but the *Jet Stream Line* requires the golfer to play *as much break* as possible, whether on the high side or the low side of the hole. Sound strange? Let me explain.

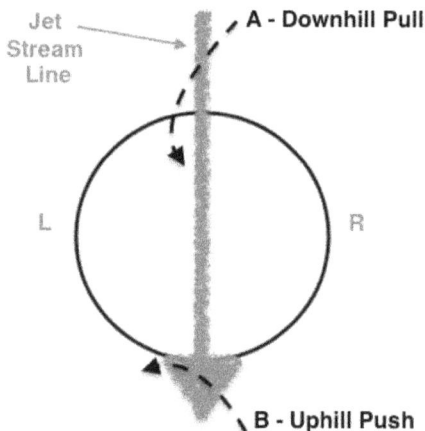

Fig. 35 The Jet Stream Line

See Fig. 35 for reference. If your ball is located on the *high side* of the hole and has break (See A), the Jet Stream Line is *your friend,* creating a slight *pull towards* the center of the cup. Crossing it is okay, even desired (within limits).

Contrastingly, if your ball is located on the *low side* of the cup and has break (See B), the Jet Stream Line is *your foe,* creating a slight *push away* from the center of the cup. Crossing it is dangerous, if not an imminent failure (within limits).

Though both scenarios seem to be opposites (uphill/downhill), both cases favor playing as much break as is intuitively possible (again, within limits). The *Jet Stream Line* approach within The Perfect Plumb Bob Method contributes to explain why so many putts are missed on the low side of the hole.

Be very aware that the straight uphill putt can easily break offline being *pushed* away by the effect of the Jet Stream Line. Be as firm as possible so that these putts are not forced offline.

There is also good news. Straight downhill putts tend to stay easily online from the *pull* of the same Jet Stream Line. As a result, straight downhill putts are difficult to miss. Keep the weight light, as the *Jetstream Line* effect carries the ball easily.

Ball-hole entry strategy is an entire subject of its own. Being able to determine the *straight putt line* will help you grow as a green reader, putt path planner, and successful putter and scorer.

(Refer to Dr. Zachary's 'SHORT PUTT Mastery' video course to learn ball-hole entry and short putt science. USE coupon code: PERFECTPLUMB at 6footer.com for a 15% discount.)

There is yet another level to move to as we progress with practise, knowledge, skill and acuity in reading slope using the Perfect Plumb Bob Method.

It's the last frontier; the last set of tools to add to your repertoire...

It's the *short cuts!*

Please visit www.6footer.com to compliment the information gained within The Perfect Plumb Bob Method.

CHAPTER 7 – SHORT CUT READS

I'm guessing that each reader must have—at some point while reading this book—asked the question, *"Do I have time to apply these techniques in a real round of golf* without delaying my group or the groups behind me?"

It's a great question—probably the most practical question to ask upon learning these skills.

Firstly, each Perfect Plumb Bobber must take notice and become aware of the time that *is available* while other players are readying to putt. Do not doddle. Prepare.

If you are first to putt, get to the green quickly and begin your read. Hole-side read first, and ball-side read second (if needed) solidifies your information on most putts. That said, time may feel tight in some circumstances—in which case, the short cuts to follow will be useful.

As you progress as a Perfect Plumb Bobber, the choice of green reading tools used will be yours. Strive to understand and become elite at all techniques in this book.

After all Perfect Plumb Bob Method techniques are learned, reading putts becomes personal. Putting is both an *art and a science*. You are the artist. And every artist is unique. All science acquired allows the artist to shine brighter.

The short cuts to follow can be used easily once one becomes proficient at setting up the main reads. Never become complacent with any of your Perfect Plumb Bob Method fundamentals. You must still develop an accurate SP and VL on every read. As you advance, setting up SP's that are on-the-putt-line or perpendicular become automatic and intuitive.

Warning: Don't get lazy when you hear the phrase *short cut*. The accurate SP remains the key to accurate reads.

In the Perfect Plumb Bob Method, there are 3 short cut categories (i.e., A, B, and C) that provide 6 useful short cut applications.

A. The HOLE-SIDE HACKS!

Short Cut #1: *The Hole-Side Break Hack*

Hole-side hacks are a method of quickly picking up an angle within the shape of the hole (the NP itself) once the proper SP and VL are established. The ability to *see* this angle will develop upon repetition. It is an advanced method for picking up slope patterns quickly and can always be further double-checked by comparing FP vs. UPSP, especially while learning the technique.

Set up your regular alignment for reading *hole-side break* (Review in Chapter 5, if needed). Hover your LPSP over the center of the hole (i.e., standard protocol). Notice how the lower shaft of the putter *slices* the shape of hole itself (See (b) in Fig. 36) as it hovers.

This *slice effect* creates an angle through the NP that can be envisioned and quickly analyzed (See (c) in Fig. 36).

An angle that deviates *counter-clockwise* from vertical indicates *a slope to the right*.

An angle that deviates *clockwise* from vertical indicates *a slope to the left*.

An angle that is perfectly *vertical* indicates *no slope* (i.e., the putt is straight or straightens at the end).

The greater the severity of the angle, the greater the slope.

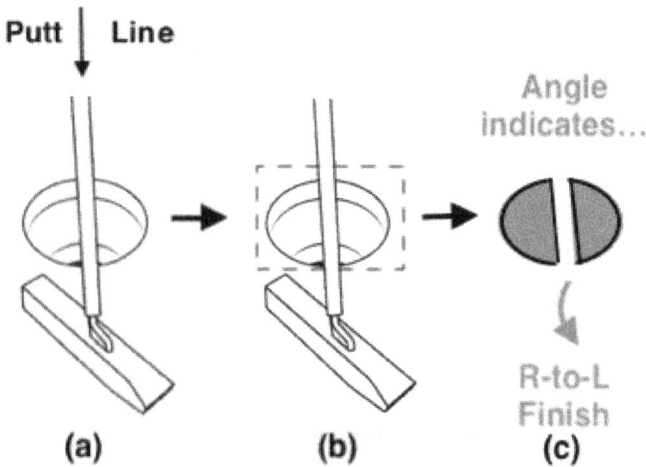

Fig. 36 (Hole-Side Break Hack)

Practise *seeing the slice angle* of the lower putter shaft through the NP. You will soon be surprised how easy it is to pick up on this angle. It is an angle that has been *hidden in plain sight* all along.

The read in Fig. 36 shows that the putt will finish with a moderate R-to-L break.

Short Cut #2: *The Hole-Side Speed Hack*

Let's use the same scenario from Fig. 36 to illustrate *the hole-side speed hack*. Notice that the only item that changes in our image example is the direction of the Putt Line (See (a) in Fig. 37).

The set up for the *hole-side speed hack* is the same as the regular *hole-side speed* read from Chapter 6 (i.e., the SP is perpendicular to the putt line). Be respectful of the putt path of fellow players.

Again, as your sense of *3-Point Alignment* becomes virtually innate, your SP is created automatically. Hover your LPSP over the NP (i.e., the hole center). Look down to notice the angular relationship with which the lower putter shaft *slices* the hole (dotted box in (b), Fig. 37). Be sure your posture does not sway lazily while performing short cut reads.

Putt Line

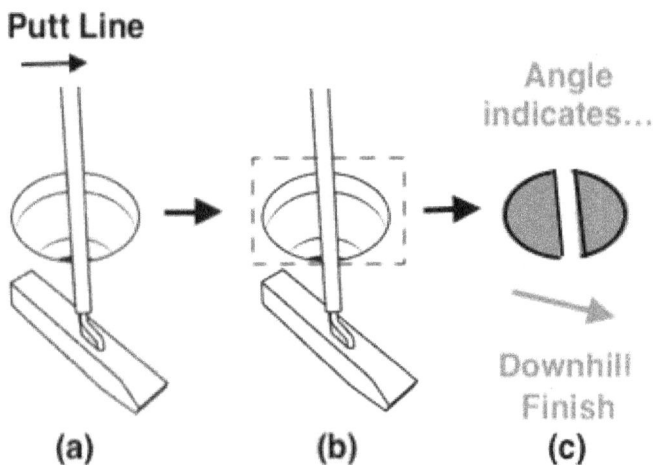

Fig. 37 (Hole-Side Speed Hack)

The counter-clockwise angle from vertical (See (c) in Fig. 37) indicates a slope to the right and therefore a moderate downhill finish to the putt represented in the example.

If the explanation above is confusing at all, please reread it a few times. Do not panic; you will understand easily upon review and practise. The short cut reads carry the same dynamics as the reads in Chapter 6.

The difference is that *short-cut reads* are evaluated relative to the lower putter shaft and the NP. If unsure, the Perfect Plumb Bobber can always double-check their findings by comparing the FP to the UPSP, as in a standard read. Remember, the SP and VL are already created.

Short Cut #3: *The Straight Putt Line Hack*

We have previously expressed the importance of being able to determine the location of the *straight putt line* (or *fault line*).

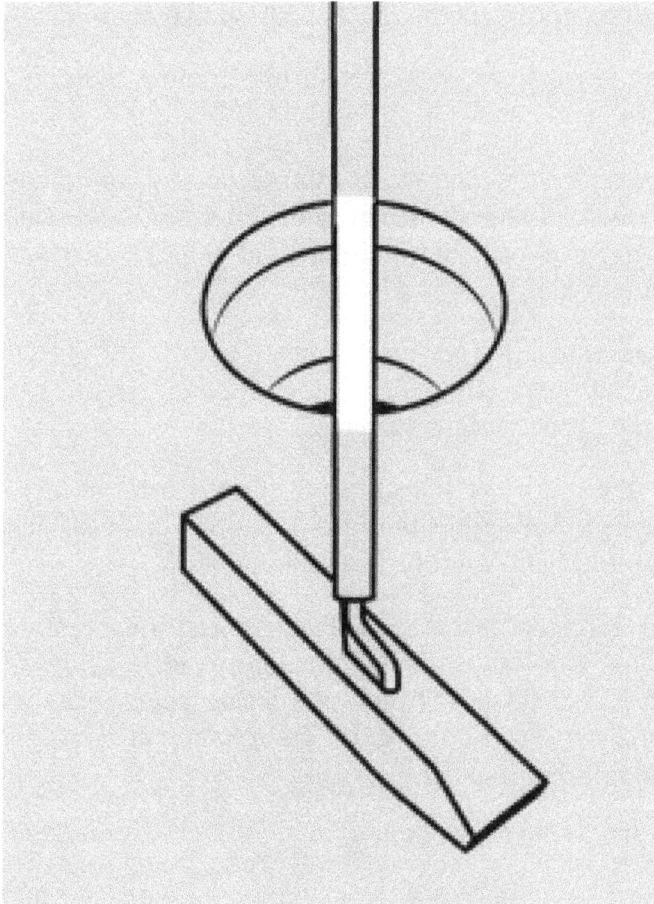

Fig. 38 (Straight Putt Line Hack)

The current short cut allows the Perfect Plumb Bobber to determine the *straight putt line* quickly.

First, ensure that you are aware of the putt paths of your playing partners.

Next, make your best guess at where the *straight putt line* might exist. Create your SP intuitively (advanced) or via step-by-step setup (i.e., align DE, NP (hole) and FP (improvise a spot, mark, or imperfection on the green along the SP)) and hover your VL over the center of the hole (NP) based on that guess.

Look at the angle with which your lower putter shaft now *slices* the middle of the hole.

Use trial and error (i.e., recall from Chapter 6, find the straight putt by moving slightly left if you find a slight left slope, and slightly right if you find a slight right slope) to determine the *straight putt line.*

The *straight putt line hack* is illustrated in Fig. 38. When the hole is dissected perfectly by the lower putter shaft, you have determined your straight putt line.

Again, the initial explanation of this short cut may seem complicated, but application and repetition of these steps will hone, simplify and solidify this technique.

Always remember that the feedback gained is quantitative and to be used as a variable. The slope being read is below the feet. Consider other factors of putt path influence, especially nearby slope and the direction of grass grain, when analyzing straight putt line information.

B. The BALL-SIDE HACKS!

Hopefully each reader has gained a genuine feel for the first 3 hole-side short cuts. The next two short cuts have the same characteristics but are observed from the ball-side. The ball is now the NP shape to consider. The ball-side hacks are explained after the hole-side hacks because they are more subtle to recognize due to the size of the golf ball/NP. It requires a more well-trained eye to recognize the angle with which the lower putter shaft *slices* the shape of the ball.

As much as the *hole-side shortcuts* were a perception stretch when compared to the 7 standard Perfect Plumb Bob Method reads, *the ball-side reads* offer another degree of challenge, attention and acuity. That said, it shouldn't take long for each reader to train their eye to see these angles.

The two *ball-side hacks* are an extension of the hole-side hacks that the reader has just learned.

Short Cut #4: *The Ball-Side Break Hack*

Refer to Fig. 39. The 3-Point alignment—and thus the SP—is the same as a regular *ball-side break* read. The NP is now the ball. Hover the lower putter shaft over the center of the ball and observe the angle with which the lower putter shaft slices the shape of the ball (Figure 39 (b)). Observe the resulting geometric shapes that remain (Figure 39 (c)) once the ball is *sliced*.

Are the shapes remaining equal/symmetrical or is there an angle made by the slice?

An angle that deviates *counter-clockwise* from vertical indicates *a slope to the right*.

An angle that deviates *clockwise* from vertical indicates *a slope to the left*.

An angle that is *vertical* indicates *no slope* (i.e., the putt is straight or starts straight).

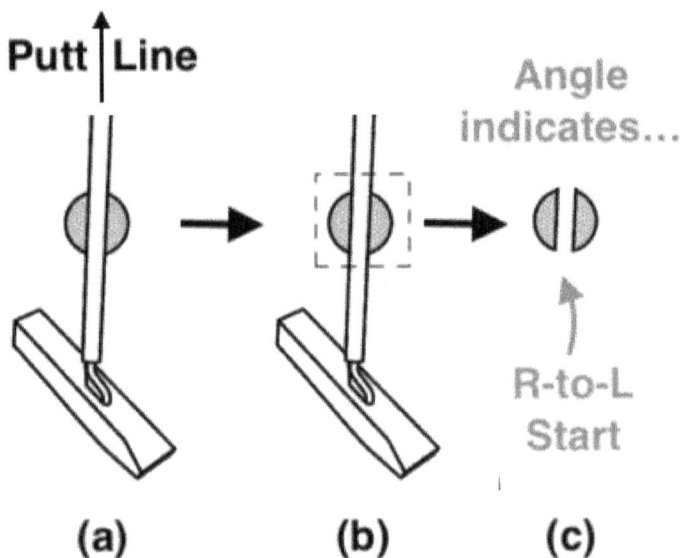

Putt|Line

Angle
indicates...

↑
R-to-L
Start

(a)　　　　(b)　　　　(c)

Fig 39 (Ball-Side Break Hack)

The greater the severity of the angle, the greater is the slope.

The read in the Fig. 39 example shows that the start of the putt has a small R-to-L break.

Short Cut #5: *The Ball-Side Speed Hack*

Let's use the same scenario from Fig. 39 to illustrate *the ball-side speed hack*. Notice that the only item that changes in our image example is the direction of the Putt Line (See (a) in Fig. 40).

The setup is for the *ball-side speed hack* is the same as the standard *ball-side speed* read from Chapter 6. You are perpendicular to the putt line. Create your SP and VL on either side of the putt line; whichever is most convenient, being respectful of the putt paths of your playing partners. Hover your LPSP over the NP (i.e., the ball). Look down to notice the angular relationship with which the lower putter shaft *slices* the ball (See the dotted box in (b), Fig. 40). Be conscious to maintain your consistent posture throughout.

Putt Line

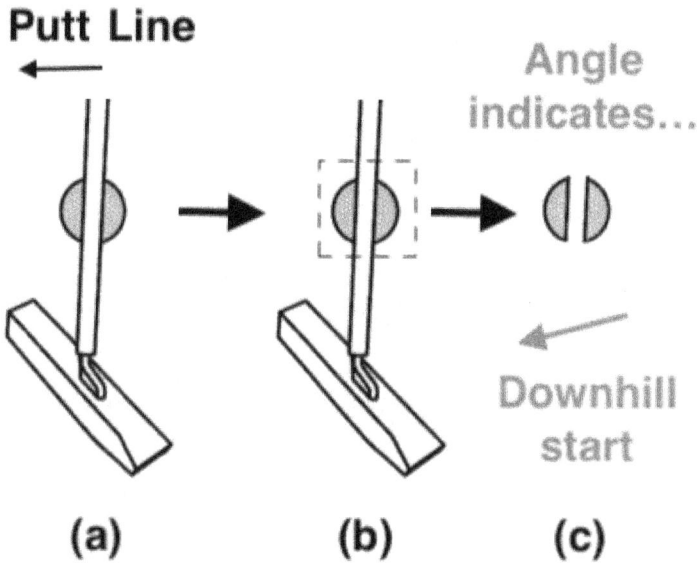

Fig. 40 (Hole-Side Speed Hack)

Are the shapes remaining (See (c) in Fig. 40) equal/symmetrical or is there an angle made by the slice?

An angle that deviates *counter-clockwise* from vertical indicates *a slope to the right.*

An angle that deviates *clockwise* from vertical indicates *a slope to the left.*

An angle that is *vertical* indicates *a neutral speed putt (i.e., neither uphill or downhill).*

The greater the severity of the angle, the greater is the slope.

The read in Fig. 40 shows a slight downhill start to the putt.

Remember, if you have any difficulty picking up on the shaft angle as it *slices* the shape of the NP on any of the *5 short cut hacks*, simply continue the standard process and perform the regular read. In other words, compare the FP and the UPSP, as the SP and VL are already set up.

It may surprise you though how quickly and acutely you see these angles after minimal practise and application.

C. The Drain Hole (DH) Hack!

The last short cut may prove to be a favorite application for Perfect Plumb Bobbers everywhere. Indeed, the drain hole hack is used regularly by the author.

Putter grip manufacturers provide a drain hole at the butt end of each putter grip which allows: 1) water to drain, 2) air to circulate, and 3) air to escape during the installation process of a new grip on a putter shaft.

This drain hole is always centered in the middle of the shaft and can thus be utilized as a true extension of the shaft center and VL.

The Perfect Plumb Bobber may simply adapt the hover height of their putter/VL during The Perfect Plumb Bob Method for any read such that the drain hole becomes the UPSP.

In other words, the drain hole is purposely positioned as the UPSP for fast, clean comparison to the FP.

View Fig. 41 to see the DH hack illustration and experiment on your own to realize the convenience, accuracy and timeliness of this hack. Your slope reading will advance in spades.

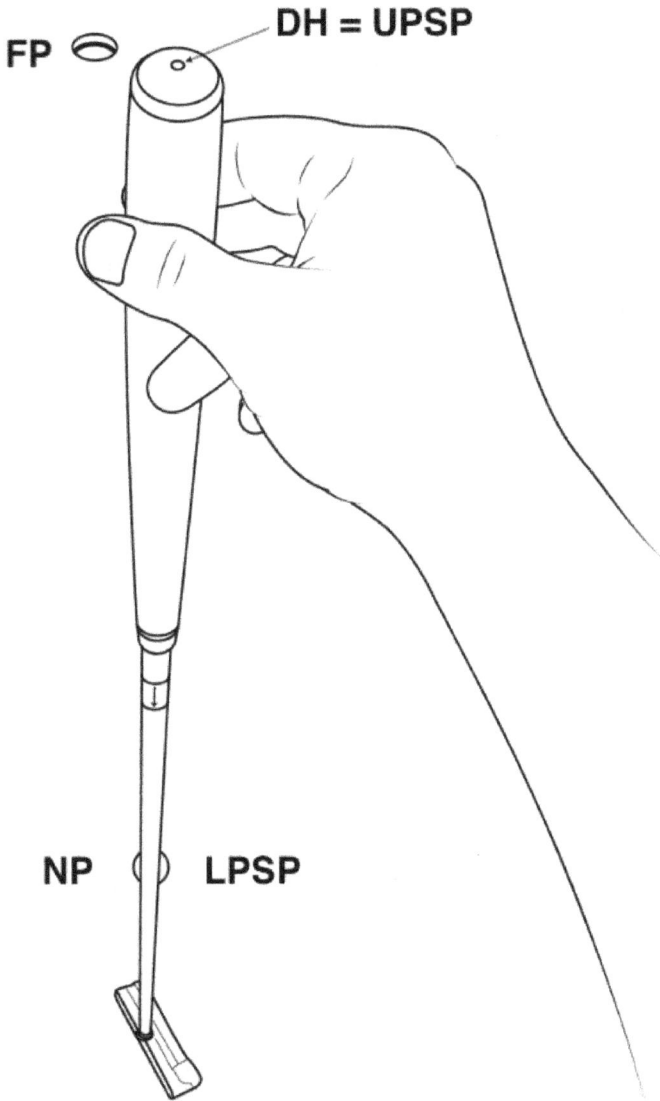

Fig. 41 The Drain Hole (DH) Hack

As mentioned, there are three great advantages to using the DH hack as part of your regular green reading procedure:

Firstly, the DH hack eliminates the problem of the putter grip body width being in the way of viewing the FP (when slopes are not large). The Perfect Plumb Bobber can *always* view the DH in comparison to the FP *immediately* on any read. With practise, it becomes easy to position the hover of the putter over the NP such that the DH and FP are easily comparable.

The second advantage of the DH hack is *accuracy*. The DH is a specific dot as opposed to a thickish area (i.e., the traditional UPSP) on a thickish line (i.e., the upper putter shaft). The Perfect Plumb Bobber can now gain immediate and precise feedback when the DH and FP are compared.

Thus, the third advantage of utilizing the DH as the UPSP is *time*. Time is always seen as a plumb bobbing challenge, so much so that it stops even the most motivated golfers from using it as a green reading tool. The Perfect Plumb Bob Method stresses the need for both timeliness and accuracy.

The innovation of the DH hack advances each golfer's skillful toolkit and makes fast, accurate plumb bobbing a reality. Try this hack and see if you don't advance *in light speed* as a green reader!

Chapter 8 will include a few example questions to quiz the Perfect Plumb Bob Method reader.

In the long term, short cuts can be used *in your regular routine, as your regular routine*, or *as a backup* or *check-up* to your standard read techniques. The choice will be yours.

Affix your mind to the views in Fig. 42 (a-f) to follow. Mentally review the slopes represented. Enjoy a brief pop quiz. The answers are posted at the beginning of Chapter 8.

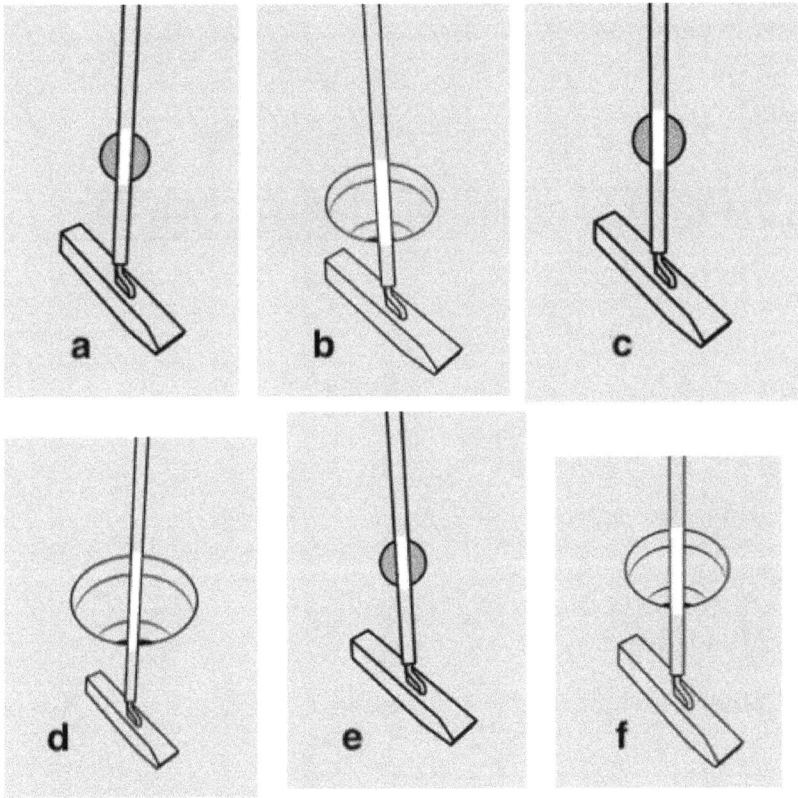

Fig. 42 (Short Cut Hacks – *Pop Quiz (Answers in Chapter 8)*)

CHAPTER 8 - PRACTISE. PRACTISE. PRACTISE.

Answers to Fig. 41 Pop Quiz (Chapter 7):

a - Mild left slope

b - Moderate right slope

c - Level

d - Mild left slope

e - Moderate right slope.

f - Level

The only barrier that now stands between you and *Perfect Plumb Bob Method Sainthood* is repetition, review, and more repetition.

Let's pique our ability to quickly recognizing slope and putt reads by testing some *real life* golf situations.

Take out a sheet of paper or guess quietly in your mind. Study the 8 slope scenarios to follow. Decide if the putt is:

a. Sloped: slight, moderate, or extreme,
b. L-to-R, R-to-L, straight, downhill, uphill, or level,
c. At the start-, finish-, or mid- of the putt.

The answers are found at the start of Chapter 9.

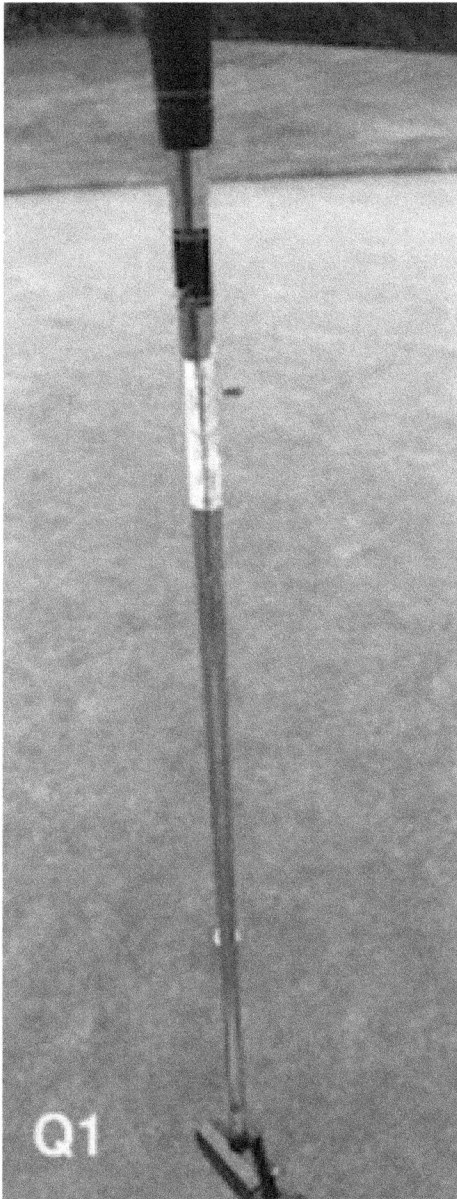

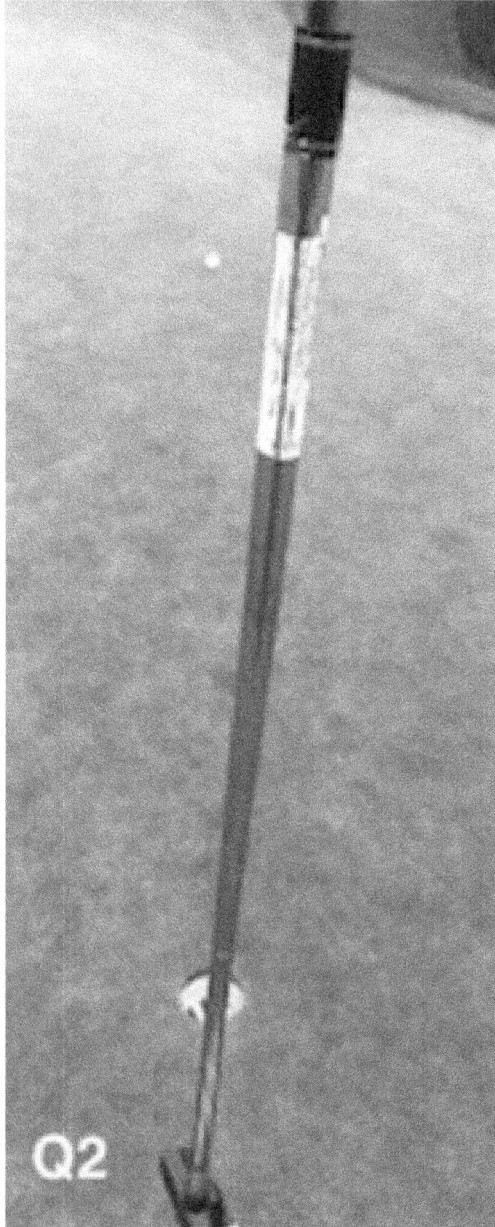

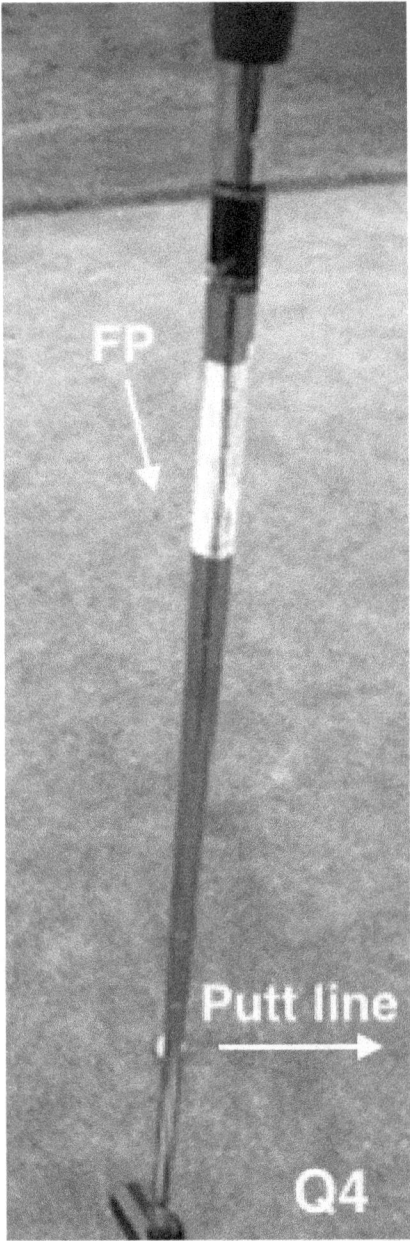

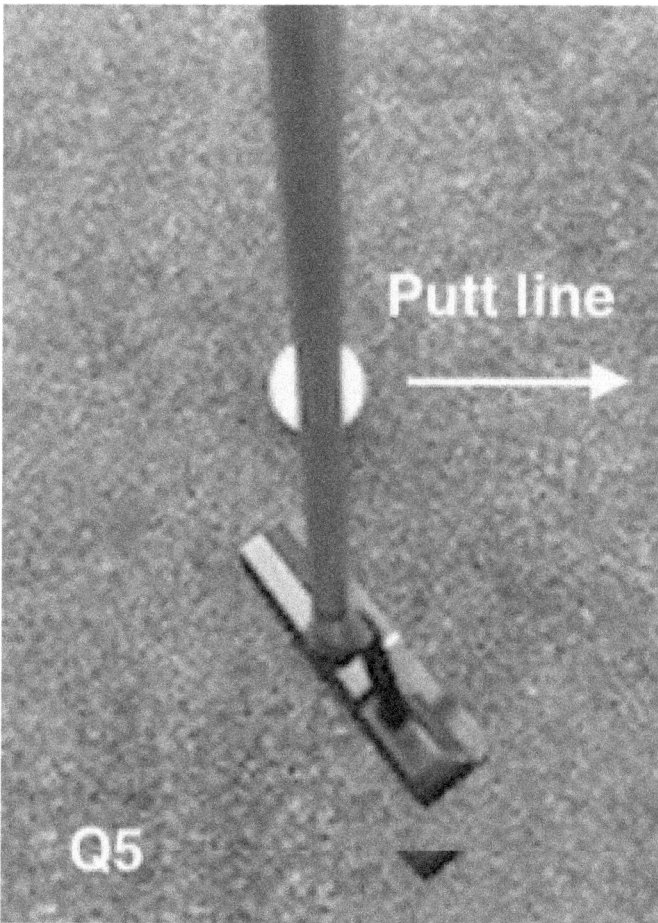

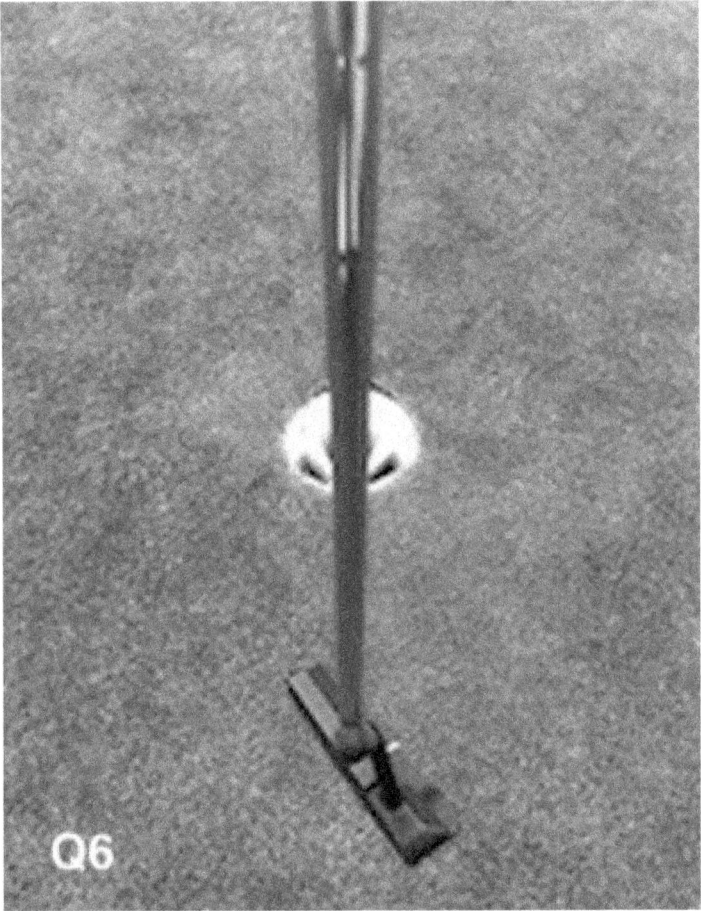

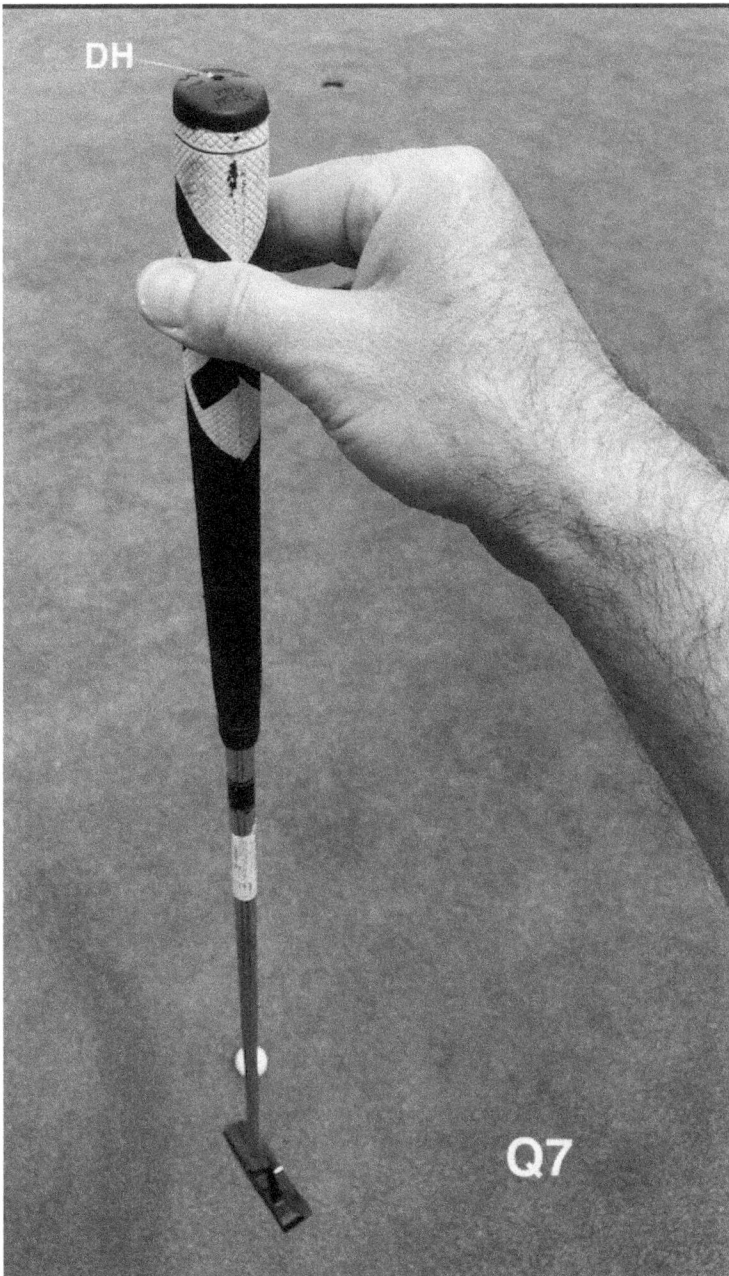

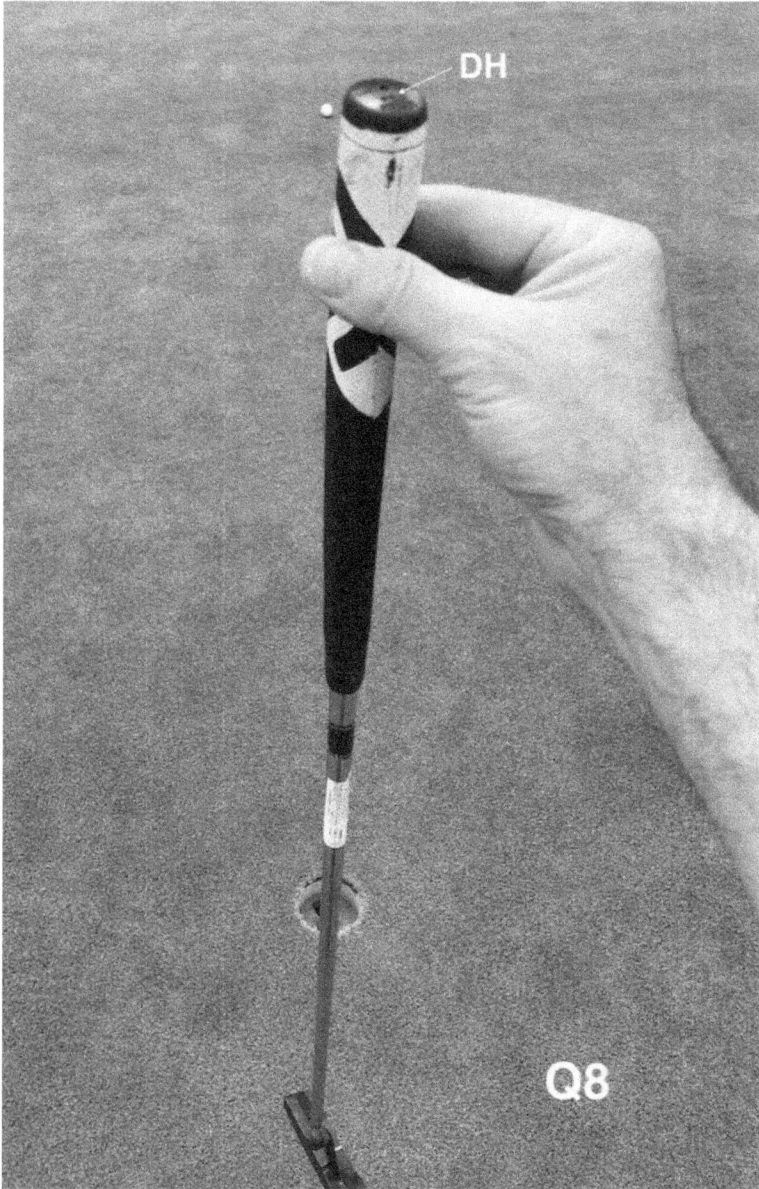

CHAPTER 9 - WHY PLUMB BOBBING WORKS

Answers from Chapter 8:

Q1. Slight L-to-R start of the putt.

Q2. Extreme L-to-R finish of the putt.

Q3. Moderate R-to-L start of the putt.

Q4. Moderate uphill slope at the start of the putt.

Q5. Slight-moderate downhill slope at the start of the putt

Q6. The straight putt line or a straight finish to the putt

Q7. Extreme L-to-R start of the putt

Q8. Slight L-to-R finish of the putt

First, let's talk about why folks have theorized that plumb bobbing *doesn't* work.

Plumb bobbing has historically been overlooked as a green-reading technique partly because many have theorized that a *stable isosceles triangle* must exist within the golfer if slopes are to be sensed accurately.

Certainly, our dominant eye (DE) cannot be on the center of our head, and thus the two sides of the triangle could never be equal. (For that matter, neither could our weaker eye be on our middle). Yet plumb bobbing, once understood, still works.

Maybe this misinterpretation was the result of seeing tripods underneath mechanical laser levels at building and highway construction sites—I'm not sure. But an isosceles triangle is not why plumb bobbing works for human-being golfers.

Human beings are not static triangular—or even square—building blocks.

Similarly, there is another thought that plumb bobbing *could not work* because individuals may have physical imbalances, such as one leg shorter than the other, a pelvic imbalance, unleveled shoulders, etc., and thus *we could not expect consistent readings.*

If this correlation were accurate (i.e., that a perfectly balanced body was required to accurately sense slope), it would be true that very few golfers would be able to plumb bob.

Indeed it is very rare to find an individual whose physical body is truly stable and balanced such that they are naturally settled onto the axis of their own vertical center. In my 10 years in private practice as a chiropractor, it was rare to see anyone enter the office whose spine was stable and well aligned. Handedness, injuries, poor/tired posture and repetitive habits all combine to contribute to this outcome. I've personally done 1000's of spinal screenings and can confidently say that few model spines exist without focused professional care.

(For complete and convenient full-body stretching, visit www.doczac.com and enroll in '**The 3-Minute Stretch**' video course. Learn it once. Own it for life. Stretch anywhere anytime. Great for daily stretching, as well as before and after golf.)

The sad fact is that proper spinal health has been largely ignored by mainstream health care, politics, and media, leaving entire populations to suffer needlessly. Miraculous changes in personal health result from simple and practical corrections to the spine—an important conversation for any day.

Fortunately for motivated golfers, it is *not* the case that perfect physical balance is required for accurate plumb bobbing.

An individual's ability to *sense level* is ultimately not a *bone and joint* apparatus alone. Instead, equilibrium is controlled by the neurological mechanisms within the vestibular system, originating from ultra-sensitive balance organs located in the inner ear.

The inner ear houses a series of fluid-filled semicircular canals that affect the linings of tiny hair-like sensors. These sensors send information to centers in the brain pertaining to balance. The brain in turn sends specific messages (via nerve networks that travel through the spinal cord) to the rest of the body, which adjusts the body to keep the inner ear fluid (and sensors) happy and level.

That is how *imbalanced* human frames *remain upright*; and it is also why every golfer has the capacity to plumb bob well (i.e., assuming that this vestibular mechanism is intact).

Let's not take this miraculous vestibular system for granted. Better general health and body balance eases the stress placed on it. Ask someone who has experienced **vertigo** just how important the vestibular system is.

Look for yourself, and start to observe head and neck tilt angles and shoulder height imbalances in your friends and family. Notice famous people in the media that you follow: online, on television, in magazines, in newspapers, etc. Are their heads tilted, or their neck and shoulders angled? Or both? Or all? You'll be doing your own spinal screenings. And professional golfers are often the worst spinal imbalance culprits.

(Note: Don't forget to check in the mirror, as well!)

Historically, we look at and communicate (with others and ourselves) while focusing on the eyes and/or mouths and lips. We overlook the relationship of the head, neck and shoulders, and thus *miss* these imbalances. Be prepared to see a lot of imbalance. You'll wonder how we humans have stayed upright at all.

But we do.

When the body unconsciously senses a slope—no matter how slight—the vestibular system becomes aware of the slope and in turn makes subtle adjustments to the rest of the body. The process is *incredibly adaptive to slope* but does not *nullify slope.*

The Perfect Plumb Bob Method picks up the subtle difference between true vertical and the body's adaptation to slope away from true vertical.

Every Perfect Plumb Bobber's body has adapted perfectly to their unique physical challenges, habits and imbalances. If you are able to stand, you are able to plumb bob.

Each Perfect Plumb Bobber's imbalance pattern is completely their own, a bit like a fingerprint. Any slope-sensing and gravity-detecting feedback will be accurate relative to one's own unique base-neutral equilibrium.

Follow the steps taught in The Perfect Plumb Bob Method properly, and feedback will be very accurate. Every now and then say *'thank you'* to the wondrous design of your vestibular system and its ability to communicate and cooperate with the rest of your body. *It is* what will be helping you make *lots of putts!*

If a Perfect Plumb Bobber decides one day to have practical and powerful corrections made to their spine and nervous system (i.e., by a certified chiropractor, physiotherapist, massage therapist, exercise specialist, etc.) rest assured, the vestibular system will update appropriately to its new base-neutral (hopefully vertical) and work just as well; likely much better.

Plus, you will experience better health and performance. Not a bad bonus.

The author strongly recommends placing priority on maintaining a healthy, stable, and balanced spine throughout life. Why? Because when the spine is imbalanced, all joints and structures of the body are at a disadvantage—and thus, they all work, weigh, and wear at a disadvantage.

The spine is the key protector of the nervous system. Why let imbalance affect your health in any way when you can keep your spine and body healthy for life?

When the spine is in balance, your body parts function best and are taxed less… including the vestibular system.

CHAPTER 10 - FINAL THOUGHTS

Two cons to mention in our summary of The Perfect Plumb Bob Method.

Wind is not our friend. It is very difficult to plumb bob in the wind, but you may see that your sense of seeing and feeling slope will have become much more acute even without plumb bobbing. The feedback gained after each experience using The Perfect Plumb Bob Method will improve your instincts. In the wind, plan your putt without the method. Pick your line. Commit to your stroke. You'll be fine. You'll be close. And remember, the wind will challenge everyone.

Delay is not our friend. Practise is absolutely essential before one takes this new act of Perfect Plumb Bobbing onto the course for a real round of golf. Spend several sessions on the practise green first. Experiment with the short cut hacks. Spend time at home and read the slopes of your floors.

The point is, get good at it. Be efficient. Be organized. Don't drive your playing partners (and others behind you) crazy.

When you have The Perfect Plumb Bob Method locked in, you should *save time* reading putts by being more decisive.

Review the standard and short cut reads from this book regularly. Ensure that you are understanding and applying all details properly. You are likely to find more information during each read-through. Be consistent in your methodical approach and posture with each read.

Guard against pre-judging slopes. Let the method speak. You will be pleasantly surprised regularly.

Yes, the steps of the Perfect Plumb Bob Method must be learned well. The application of the reads learned is really up to you, the golfer. The author believes that if golfers would adopt a consistent routine of quickly reading putts from both the hole-side and the ball-side, they would *see the putt better*—and *make much more of them.*

You now have the skills to do just that, accurately and quickly. Often, putts are obvious and one (or no) plumb bob read may suffice. Be sensible. Be confident. Often the break of your putt will be obvious via watching another player's putt in your group.

As with all new skills, do not expect results immediately. You may feel uncomfortable in the beginning. You may not feel like a Perfect Plumb Bobber at all. Stick with it. Be persistent. Be patient. Hone your skills.

You will begin to see subtleties you have never noticed before on putting greens. You will notice optical illusions and deceptions regularly. You will also know if you have made a bad stroke or misread the putt. Pay attention. All putts are learning experiences. All putts give feedback. All feedback has the potential to make us better.

Poor putt path planning is the #1 reason for missing putts. Always evaluate your putt path strategy in order to evolve. Are you consistently playing too little or too much break? Is your weight too light or too heavy? Adjust as needed.

Remember that slope, though essential, is but one ingredient within the full recipe of reading the path of a putt. It is akin to *the batter of the cake.*

You must also be aware of grain & grass conditions, drainage, sun direction, time of day, green speed, temperature, wear, and wind direction. All are subtle components of a final computation. Strive to research and improve your awareness of all.

Enroll in Dr. Zachary's **SHORT PUTT Mastery™** video course at http://www.6footer.com to advance your knowledge, approach and skill regarding short putting, including complete green reading. Become a master short putter and watch your scores sink low and your enjoyment for the game rise up.

Order Dr. Zachary's putting aids, 1) **PUTT Ramp™** (use indoor & outdoor to learn hole entry & have fun while practicing), 2) **MONEYBALL™**, 3) **PUTT Port™** at http://www.6footer.com Perfect for home, office & putting green use.

Learn Dr. Zachary's **The 3-Minute Stretch™** so that you can remain strong, flexible, and balanced throughout your life. Great to keep you fit to read greens in a standing or squatting position. Great for your golf and any other recreation. Great for your health. Learn it once. Own it for life. Fast, easy daily stretching. Visit: http://www.doczac.com

Whatever your final putt plan is on each putt, ***commit to your putting stroke.*** Indecisiveness is the second biggest reason for low putts-made percentages. You'll make more than your share of putts (and learn more) when you are 1) confident in your read and 2) committed to your stroke.

The Perfect Plumb Bob Method is not intended to develop cocky egotists. Instead, it is designed to develop well-educated green readers and well-rounded golfers that create their very best putt path plans for their very best scoring.

Ultimately, the goal of The Perfect Plumb Bob Method is to further expose golfers (and soon-to-be golfers) to the wonders of the great game of golf. So many play the game on a superficial level keeping it at arm's length and floating over the many fascinating intricacies and lessons within.

Dig deep at learning and applying The Perfect Plumb Bob Method. Dig deep at advancing your entire game. Golf will never bore you. Golf will never let you get carried away about *how great you* are—or *how poor you are*. There's always more to learn.

Maybe The Perfect Plumb Bob Method will even expose golfers to the *perfection* of *Nature,* a nature we are all well a part of.

Welcome, new Perfect Plumb Bobber!

Best wishes in your pursuit of better performance and lower golf scores!

See you somewhere down the slope!

THE END

(& The Beginning of Your Perfect

Plumb Bob Method Journey)

"The best way to handle pressure is to establish a pre-putt routine and never deviate from it. It should be automatic, freeing your mind so you can focus on the task at hand."

Tiger Woods

"The stroke itself is a minor, almost insignificant, part of putting. Much more critical are consistent setup, reading greens and—most important of all—aiming the clubface correctly."

Phil Mickelson

Readers of The Perfect Plumb Bob Method may also enjoy **The Power of Golf** by Dr. Terry Zachary that explores a young golfer's journey from enthusiastic junior golfer to student of the games of golf and life. For golfers young and old, beginner to advanced.

The Power of Golf is based on Dr. Zachary's real-life experiences travelling with and treating professional golfers, as well as his time in private health care practice.

The Power of Golf is available (at Amazon) in eBook, soft cover, hard cover, and (at Audible) in audiobook.